FOOLS' PARADISE

The Voyage of a Ship of Fools
from Europe

A Mock-Heroic Poem on Brexit

JOHN HUNT PUBLISHING

First published by O-Books, 2020
O-Books is an imprint of John Hunt Publishing Ltd., No. 3 East St., Alresford, Hampshire SO24 9EE, UK
office@jhpbooks.com
www.johnhuntpublishing.com

For distributor details and how to order please visit the 'Ordering' section on our website.

Text copyright: Nicholas Hagger 2019

ISBN: 978 1 78904 275 7
978 1 78904 276 4 (ebook)
Library of Congress Control Number: 2019945273

A CIP catalogue record for this book is available from the British Library.

Design: Stuart Davies

UK: Printed and bound by CPI Group (UK) Ltd, Croydon, CR0 4YY
US: Printed and bound by Thomson-Shore, 7300 West Joy Road, Dexter, MI 48130

We operate a distinctive and ethical publishing philosophy in all areas of our business, from our global network of authors to production and worldwide distribution.

FOOLS' PARADISE

The Voyage of a Ship of Fools from Europe

A Mock-Heroic Poem on Brexit

Nicholas Hagger

BOOKS

Winchester, UK
Washington, USA

Also by Nicholas Hagger

The Fire and the Stones
Selected Poems
The Universe and the Light
A White Radiance
A Mystic Way
Awakening to the Light
A Spade Fresh with Mud
The Warlords
Overlord
A Smell of Leaves and Summer
The Tragedy of Prince Tudor
The One and the Many
Wheeling Bats and a Harvest Moon
The Warm Glow of the Monastery Courtyard
The Syndicate
The Secret History of the West
The Light of Civilization
Classical Odes
Overlord, one-volume edition
Collected Poems 1958–2005
Collected Verse Plays
Collected Stories
The Secret Founding of America
The Last Tourist in Iran
The Rise and Fall of Civilizations
The New Philosophy of Universalism
The Libyan Revolution
Armageddon
The World Government
The Secret American Dream
A New Philosophy of Literature
A View of Epping Forest
My Double Life 1: This Dark Wood
My Double Life 2: A Rainbow over the Hills

Selected Stories: Follies and Vices of the Modern Elizabethan Age
Selected Poems: Quest for the One
The Dream of Europa
The First Dazzling Chill of Winter
Life Cycle and Other New Poems 2006–2016
The Secret American Destiny
Peace for our Time
World State
World Constitution
King Charles the Wise
Visions of England

"The man of letters as such, is not concerned with the political or economic map of Europe; but he should be very much concerned with its cultural map.... The man of letters... should be able to take a longer view than either the politician or the local patriot.... The cultural health of Europe, including the cultural health of its component parts, is incompatible with extreme forms of both nationalism and internationalism.... The responsibility of the man of letters at the present time... should be vigilantly watching the conduct of politicians and economists, for the purpose of criticizing and warning, when the decisions and actions of the politicians and economists are likely to have cultural consequences. Of these consequences the man of letters should qualify himself to judge. Of the possible cultural consequences of their activities, politicians and economists are usually oblivious; the man of letters is better qualified to foresee them, and to perceive their seriousness."

T.S. Eliot, *The Man of Letters and the Future of Europe*, 1944

"Poetry and politics.... Poetry is art, which involves seeing all sides of a question in depth. Politics is about getting things done and generally involves a point of view, which in poetry can appear to be propaganda unless it's treated in a rounded way and not in black-white, right-wrong terms."

Nicholas Hagger, letter to Sir John Weston, 1 February 2010

"O God of earth and altar,
Bow down and hear our cry,
Our earthly rulers falter,
Our people drift and die."

G.K. Chesterton, A Hymn: 'O God of Earth and Altar', 1906

"Day after day, day after day,
We stuck, nor breath nor motion;
As idle as a painted ship
Upon a painted ocean."

Samuel Coleridge, 'The Ancient Mariner', 1798

"Lo! thy dread empire, Chaos! is restored;
Light dies before thy uncreating word;
Thy hand, great Anarch! lets the curtain fall,
And universal darkness buries all."

Alexander Pope, The Dunciad, bk IV, lines 653–656, 1742/43

"'Fool', a person who acts unwisely or imprudently; a stupid person."
"'Fool's paradise', happiness founded on an illusion."

Concise Oxford Dictionary

"A fool's paradise is a wise man's hell."

Thomas Fuller, *The Holy State and the Profane State*,
book 4, chapter 20, 1642

"A limbo large and broad, since call'd
The Paradise of Fools to few unknown."

John Milton, *Paradise Lost*, book III, lines 495–496, 1667

"It is better to be unhappy and know the worst, than to be happy in a fool's paradise!"

Fyodor Dostoevsky, *The Idiot*, Part 4, chapter 5, 1869

"Do not feel envious of the happiness of those who live in a fool's paradise, for only a fool will think that it is happiness."

Bertrand Russell, 'A Liberal Decalogue' in *New York Times Magazine*,
16 December 1951 (and later in *The Autobiography of Bertrand Russell*,
Vol. 3, 1944–1967)

"Get beyond all difference and conflict to the unity behind all diversity."

Bede Griffiths in conversation with Nicholas Hagger over
breakfast, Nicholas Hagger's diary for 12 April 1992,
My Double Life 2: A Rainbow over the Hills, p.389

The front cover shows a woodcut thought to be by Albrecht Dürer in *The Ship of Fools* (*Das Narrenschiff*), a German poem by the German humanist Sebastian Brant published in Basel, Switzerland in 1494. Above the image in the Latin version by Jakob Locher in 1497 are the Latin words *Stultifera Navis*, 'fool-bearing ship'. On either side within the image are the Latin words *navis* ('ship') and *stultoru[m]* ('of fools'). In a later English version a caption beneath in English says 'The Ship of Fools Bids Farewell to Europe'. (See pp.xxvi and xxviii.)

A corner-mark (⌐) at the beginning of the line denotes that there is a break or gap before that line which has been obscured because it falls at the bottom of a page.

CONTENTS

Preface to *Fools' Paradise*:
The Mock-Heroic Tradition

Social satire

The first tutorial I had with Christopher Ricks in the early summer of 1959, 60 years ago, he took me out to a seat in the Worcester College gardens on a warm summer morning and asked me what poems I liked. I said, "Mystical poems about the universe as in Wordsworth, Blake and Shelley." He said, "I shall teach you to like social satire." From the very outset we had different casts of mind but I was open to his guidance and embraced Swift, Dryden and Pope.

The tradition of mock-heroic verse

The tradition of mock-heroic verse is a long one. It looks back to the elevated heroic style of the classical epic poems of Homer (*The Iliad* and *The Odyssey*) and Virgil (*The Aeneid*) and more recently Milton's *Paradise Lost*, all of which were unrhymed, and adapts it to a trivial subject to suggest the unheroic character of the modern age. It satirises epic poetry, and it arguably began with an anonymous burlesque of Homer's *The Iliad* in the ancient world, *Batrachomyomachia* (*Battle of the Frogs and the Mice*), which was perhaps written in the 4th century BC but may not have been written until the 2nd century AD. In the battle between the frogs and the mice Zeus proposes that the gods take sides and tries to persuade Athena to help the mice.

In English Literature social satire looks back to the narrative poems of Chaucer. The naïve narrators in *The Book of the Duchess* (1368–1369) and *The House of Fame* (1378–1381) satirise the narrator-guide relationship of Dante and Virgil in Dante's *Divine Comedy* (1308–1320). *The Parliament of Birds* (*Parlement of Foules*, 1378–1381) satirises the social classes, which are represented by different birds. Chaucer lived on the fringe of political intrigue and was very alert to the politics of his day, having in 1366 married the sister (Philippa Roet) of Katharine Swynford, the love of the Lancastrian John of Gaunt's life and last wife, and having held public office during the power struggle between the Houses of Lancaster and York for the succession after Edward III's death in 1377, which led to the Wars of the Roses. (Gaunt's son eventually became Henry IV.)

The tradition of mock-heroic being applied to English politicians in English literature looks back to Dryden's 'Absalom and Achitophel' (1681), which is in rhymed heroic couplets. It deals in allegorical form (scriptural disguises) with Lord Shaftesbury's party's attempt to exclude the Duke of York from the succession and replace him with the Duke of Monmouth. Dryden wrote the poem to influence the outcome (then in the balance) by revealing the true characters of the politicians he described, most notably Shaftesbury (the false tempter Achitophel) and Monmouth (Absalom).

The mock-heroic approach was adopted by 'modern' writers seeking to ridicule contemporary classicists, the 'ancients', as in Nicolas Boileau's mock-heroic poem *'Le Lutrin'* ('The Lectern', 1674–1683) in which a quarrel between two ecclesiastics about where to place a lectern in a chapel ends in a battle in a bookstore, with books by 'ancient' and 'modern' authors being flung about by the two ecclesiastics. Jonathan Swift varied this theme in 'The Battle of the Books', part of the *prolegomena* to *A Tale of a Tub* (1704), which is in mock-heroic prose.

Alexander Pope's 'The Rape of the Lock' (1712–1714) is in heroic couplets. It was first published in two cantos and then enlarged to five cantos. It describes a society beau's trivial cutting of a lock of hair from the head of a society belle as if it were comparable to the abduction of Helen which began the Trojan War. Lord Petre cuts a lock of Miss Arabella Fermor's hair, causing a quarrel between the two families, and Pope seeks to allay this quarrel on the model of Boileau's *'Le Lutrin'*. He shows Belinda (Arabella Fermor) at her dressing-table, at a game of *ombre*, and drinking coffee, when her lock is snipped. He shows her wrath and describes how the lock becomes a new star in the sky.

The first two versions of Pope's mock-heroic poem *The Dunciad* ('book of dunces'), bks I–III, were published anonymously in 1728 and 1729, and Pope acknowledged authorship in 1735. Bk IV was added in 1742 and a revised version of all four books was published in 1743. *The Dunciad* celebrates the goddess Dulness and the progress of her chosen dunces (including many of his contemporary poets), who filled Great Britain with chaotic ignorance and tasteless drivel.

My interpretation of the mock-heroic tradition
I came to mock-heroic after writing my epic poem *Overlord* (1994–1996),

which is about the Second World War from D-Day to the Fall of Berlin, with Eisenhower as its hero (41,000 lines of blank verse); and again after the publication of my second epic poem, *Armageddon* (2008–2009), which is about the War on Terror after 9/11, especially the wars in Afghanistan and Iraq, with George W. Bush as its hero (25,000 lines of blank verse). Having adopted an elevated tone in these two epics I was able to use epic devices such as invocations to the Muse and supernatural interventions in my mock-heroic.

In my interpretation of mock-heroic I have followed Dryden's focus on politics but have drawn on Pope's social satire. In 2000 I wrote 'Zeus's Ass' in seven cantos about UK Prime Minister Blair's vacuity and spin. It focuses on Blair's being barracked by an audience of women, all members of the Women's Institute. In 'Zeus's Emperor' (2009/2015, three cantos) I focused on Blair's attempt to be appointed the next President of the European Council ('EU President') in 2009, a post that went to Herman Van Rompuy. Both these poems have political overtones, and they are modern attempts to write in the tradition of Dryden's 'Absalom and Achitophel' and Pope's 'The Rape of the Lock' and *The Dunciad* in rhymed heroic couplets.

In *Fools' Paradise* I have followed the mock-heroic tradition by writing in heroic couplets (rhyming couplets) in iambic pentameters, as in 'Zeus's Ass' and 'Zeus's Emperor'. My basic foot is of course the iamb ($\cup$ –), but I have been alert to stress and when the sense has required I have resorted to trochees (– $\cup$), anapaests ($\cup$ $\cup$ –) and dactyls (– $\cup$ $\cup$), and occasionally to amphibrachs ($\cup$ – $\cup$). My poetic notation has been adapted to the demands of conveying international negotiations and the conflicts surrounding them.

In his preface to *Paradise Lost* under a heading *The Verse* Milton champions "English heroic verse without rime, as that of Homer in Greek, and of Virgil in Latin" and laments "the troublesome and modern bondage of riming" which is "the invention of a barbarous age, to set off wretched matter and lame metre". In my two epic poems, *Overlord* and *Armageddon*, I have agreed with Milton's analysis and used unrhymed blank verse, but in 'Zeus's Ass', 'Zeus's Emperor' and now *Fools' Paradise* I have followed the mock-heroic convention established by Dryden and Pope and have submitted myself to the "troublesome… bondage" of rhyme. I have sought to avoid lame metre by varying my iambic feet with trochees, anapaests, dactyls and amphibrachs. I would not disagree that the matter, which has presented itself in the news of the last two-and-a-half years, is "wretched".

Fools' Paradise

In *Fools' Paradise* I focus on Brexit, the most important decision the UK has taken since the declaration of the Second World War, and in particular on the promises of the Brexiteers which led to the referendum's being won by Leave and the non-delivery of their promises and the chaos they caused. Following my presentation of leaders in my other works – Eisenhower and Hitler, George W. Bush and bin Laden, Blair and Van Rompuy – I present the Chequers gathering at which the Chequers proposal was first introduced, the subsequent resignation of two leading Brexiteers, and the slide towards 'no deal' with a hostile European Union being unsympathetic to the British proposal, and the delays to leaving and long-term prospect of staying-in. I show the divisions within the Conservative party and in the country, and the chaotic May leadership which could not enforce collective Cabinet responsibility.

The Conservative leadership and, indeed, the politicians of all parties in Westminster seemed to be unable to agree on what course to take, in what direction the UK public should be led, and lurking behind the poem is the 1494 poem *Ship of Fools* by Sebastian Brant (published in Basel, Switzerland), which describes a voyage of fools who possess all the follies and vices of their time to Narragonia, the Fools' Paradise, which does not exist except in the minds of the captain and the crew. The caption under a later English version of the woodcut of *Ship of Fools* (see p.xxvii) states that they were bidding "farewell to Europe".

The idea of a ship making a daft voyage is based on Plato's comparison of a philosopher being ignored by society to a ship's captain being ignored by his dysfunctional crew in *The Republic* book 6 (c.380BC), which I had to read in Greek at school. As Plato's description originated the allegory of a Ship of Fools with a dysfunctional crew and also the metaphor of the Ship of State – which was anticipated in the poetry of Alcaeus of Mytilene (621–560), Aeschylus's *Seven Against Thebes* (c.467BC) and Sophocles' *Antigone* (c.441BC) – it is worth quoting:

Suppose the following to be the state of affairs on board a ship or ships.

The captain is larger and stronger than any of the crew, but a bit deaf and short-sighted, and doesn't know much about navigation. The crew are all quarrelling with each other about how to navigate the ship, each thinking he ought to be at the helm; they know no navigation and cannot say that anyone ever taught it them, or that they spent any time studying it; indeed they say it can't be taught and are ready to murder anyone who says it can. They spend all their time milling round the captain and trying to get him to give them the wheel. If one faction is more successful than another, their rivals may kill them and throw them overboard, lay out the honest captain with drugs or drink, take control of the ship, help themselves to what's on board, and behave as if they were on a drunken pleasure-cruise. Finally, they reserve their admiration for the man who knows how to lend a hand in controlling the captain by force or fraud; they praise his seamanship and navigation and knowledge of the sea and condemn everyone else as useless. They have no idea that the true navigator must study the seasons of the year, the sky, the stars, the winds and other professional subjects, if he is to be really fit to control a ship; and they think that it's quite impossible to acquire professional skill in navigation (quite apart from whether they want it exercised) and that there's no such thing as an art of navigation. In these circumstances aren't the sailors on any such ship bound to regard the true navigator as a gossip and a star-gazer, of no use to them at all?

In the woodcut of *Ship of Fools* the captain, crew and passengers all wear jester's hats and the captain is on the prow pointing forward and calling to the other fools. They are not looking at him or listening to him, they are too busy pushing a fool overboard or drinking wine, and those at the helm at the rear of the ship have their back to him and are steering in a different direction. The fools are already fighting among themselves, and mutiny is not far off. It is a truly chaotic voyage.

The metaphor of Plato's ship was carried forward by Horace's Ship of State in troubled waters (*Odes* 1.14) and in more modern poetry such as Longfellow's "Sail on, O Ship of State" in 'The Building of the Ship' (quoted by Churchill in a speech on 13 April 1941).

Brexit

The British attempt to 'exit the European Union' has dominated the newspapers since the 2016 UK referendum. In 2017 44% of the UK's trade (worth £274 billion) was with the EU, the most significant trading bloc in the world. The UK electorate voted to walk away from half the UK's income to make better trading arrangements with the US, India, China and the Commonwealth countries. Continuing alignment with the EU would make these new trading arrangements impossible. However continuing alignment with the EU seemed inevitable as the only way to preserve a frictionless border between Northern Ireland and the EU without turning the Irish Sea into a border, separating Northern Ireland from the rest of the UK and breaking the UK up and without encouraging Scotland to declare independence, was to remain in the EU. Consequently the UK could not agree on how to implement the new trading arrangements. The European Commission was disinclined to reach a deal with the UK as it did not want any of the other 27 member-states following the UK's example and breaking away.

The momentum in the EU was now for more integration and for allowing more European nation-states to join. With Russia threatening the Baltic states a United States of Europe was looming with its own army and defence, and it seemed that the UK had turned towards isolationism at a time when most European nation-states were preparing to resist a menacing Russia. The UK seemed to be sailing against the tide of history. The negotiations led to an *impasse* and parallels were drawn with the miscalculation that led to the Suez crisis, which lasted for several weeks.

Today the world order seems to be breaking down – hence the momentum for integration within the EU. The US, leader of the West for most of the 20th century, has turned inwards and unpredictable and stands for 'America First'. Putin menaces unpredictably on Europe's eastern front. China is showing signs of expansionism in the South China Sea and in Africa, and is engaging in a trade war with the US. To believe that the UK can have a greater influence on world events on its own than it could as part of the integrationist EU when the world order is breaking down is seen by many to be a fantasy.

Essentially Brexit has been a battleground between conflicting ideologies: between supranationalism and nationalism. Neither Brexit nor

Trump's nationalistic isolationism will deflect the rise of a coming World State.

Dialectic between opposites

As I wrote in the Preface to my masque *King Charles the Wise*, in all my works there is a dialectic in which two opposites are reconciled in a unity in accordance with the algebraic formula I found when living in the East, $+A + -A = 0$. My two masques conform to a dialectic involving disorder and order. *The Dream of Europa* celebrated 70 years of peace achieved by the EU; and *King Charles the Wise* celebrated the UK's new global role that could lead to universal peace. Both contradictory masques would be reconciled within a coming World State.

I pointed out that *King Charles the Wise*'s view of the UK's post-Brexit future would be contradicted by *Fools' Paradise*, which would be about the UK's departure from the European Union. I said that both would be reconciled within a coming World State. It is worth quoting my exact words to make my message clear:

> Similarly, this masque about the UK's post-Brexit future, *King Charles the Wise*, will be contradicted by its opposite, a mock-heroic long poem in progress about the circumstances surrounding the UK's departure from the European Union, *Fools' Paradise*, and both are similarly reconciled within the World State.

I did not start writing the "long poem in progress" until 7 August 2018. I wrote the first five cantos and the first two sections of canto VI in Charlestown, Cornwall between 7 and 17 August 2018. The poem was only supposed to be seven cantos like 'Zeus's Ass'. I was clear that I should start with the Chequers plan but Prime Minister May's delaying kept prolonging the negotiations and therefore my poem, and I needed to wait for the outcome. I wrote the last six cantos and the Epilogue between August and December 2018 and rhymed from some way into canto IX to the third section of canto XII between 19 December 2018 and 1 January 2019. I added cantos XIII and XIV and redistributed the text of cantos XI–XIV to even out the length of the sections on 30 January 2019, added more in February and March and completed the poem on 12 April. I redistributed the text of cantos XIII and XIV to even the length in the evening of 12 April. I completed these amendments on 16 April 2019. On 3 May to even the length I redistributed the text of canto XIII into cantos XIII and XIV, and the text of canto XIV into cantos XV and XVI.

In *Fools' Paradise* I present the Brexiteers – and all the politicians – as being on a Ship of Fools. Both *King Charles the Wise* and *Fools' Paradise* would have their contradictions reconciled within a coming World State. In my ongoing dialectic of opposites I am following a method Blake used: his *Songs of Innocence* and *Songs of Experience* contained opposite views (symbolised by the innocent gentle lamb and the experienced savage tiger) which were fundamentally reconciled in the underlying unity that contains both.

So am I for or against Brexit? I am neither. I present both sides in *King Charles the Wise* and *Fools' Paradise*. I am like the reporter who is sent to the Emirates Stadium to report on Arsenal's latest home match and reflects what happens with a degree of objectivity. I may be an Arsenal supporter, but in my report I am balanced and present an objective view of the performance of both sides in the game. Although Brexiteers may be aggrieved by the mock-heroic tone of this work and by my dwelling on the Ship of Fools, they will find their case presented in my work as a whole, for example in the words of Britannia in *King Charles the Wise*. I look beyond the pros and cons of Brexit for both are ultimately reconciled within a World State.

The UK belongs to the European civilisation
In *The Fire and the Stones* and later in *The Rise and Fall of Civilizations* I have shown that the UK belongs to the European civilisation. The UK and the European nation-states share a common heritage in belonging to the Roman Empire and in medieval Catholicism and the Reformation. I show that 25 civilisations, including the European civilisation, all pass through 61 similar stages and share a unified pattern. They rise and fall in a rainbow-like parabola. I show that they rise round their 'central idea', a metaphysical vision of the Fire or Light that is embodied in religion and reflected in European literature by poets such as Dante, Milton, the Metaphysical poets and T.S. Eliot, and they fall through secularisation.

During this fall they pass into my stage 43, a Union (in the case of the

European civilisation currently the European Union), and stage 44, in which there is syncretism as religious sects draw together in the shadow of a new conglomerate (the EU) and espouse Universalism, which in one of its tenets sees the Fire or Light as the common source of all religions.

In stage 45 there is a rejection of the present, a reassertion of the national perspective, a yearning for the nation's lost past and a revival of cultural purity as has happened in the Arab world with IS's longing to return to the 7th century AD – and, in a less violent way, in the UK with Brexiteers' longing to opt out of the European civilisation and return to the conditions of the British Empire. In stage 46 civilisations pass into a federation. In our time the Soviet Union passed into the Russian Federation, and eventually the European Union will pass into the European Federation, as the United Kingdom can be expected to do. (I wrote in *The Fire and the Stones*, 1991, of the "dismemberment of the United Kingdom when Ireland is reunited with the European conglomerate", and it remains to be seen whether in view of the backstop this was prophetic.)

The role of the true poet

The true poet timelessly reflects the central idea of his civilisation even when the civilisation is in decline and heading for its end (when it will be absorbed into another civilisation as the ancient Mesopotamian and Egyptian civilisations were absorbed into the Islamic Arab civilisation). The true poet stands apart from society even more than the Church and channels the mystic Fire or Light into his civilisation in his poems. The true poet – such as Dante, Milton, the Metaphysical poets, the Augustan and Romantic poets, and T.S. Eliot – beams metaphysical Reality into his society, and does not shrink from criticising the aims and goals of the Government of the day as I did in *The Dream of Europa* and *King Charles the Wise*, and do now in *Fools' Paradise*.

The role of the true European poet is to be a truth-bearer in a mendacious Age, to make a principled stand for true values and to reflect the driving force and central idea of European society to its regional readers. In the past poets have been exiled by their civilisation's rulers for telling the truth as in the Roman civilisation Ovid was exiled by Augustus, which I covered in my verse play *Ovid Banished*. The role of the true poet is not to flatter those in authority but to hold them to account for their misdeeds, using the time-honoured, tried-and-tested form of social satire. Both Byron (in the 'Dedication' to *Don Juan*) and Shelley attacked Castlereagh, the British Foreign Secretary and Leader of the House of Commons from 1812 to 1822.

The true European poet uses language in a truthful and unmendacious way, which conflicts with politicians' bland and deceptive use of language. I knew Sir John Biggs-Davison for many years. He succeeded Winston Churchill as my MP and sent me a ticket to hear Prime Minister Eden speak in the main Suez debate in the Commons on 12 September 1956. He invited me to the Commons on many occasions and said I had had experience in Libya and elsewhere that would be valuable in the House, and on several occasions hinted that one day I might become his successor. When he announced his impending retirement due to ill health in 1988 he asked me via an intermediary if I wanted my name to go forward to succeed him. I said no. I had more than fifty books to write and I had chosen to be an author and for me that was the right decision. I knew that Andrew Marvell was an MP at various times between 1659 and 1678 as well as a Metaphysical poet, but I would not have been happy to use language to obfuscate as politicians often do, as a smokescreen. The true poet uses language to reflect experience with clarity and, although ambiguity and verbal play have a place in poetry, conveys experience of the universe with integrity and is wary of politicians' dissembling language.

I wrote about the role of the poet in my letter to Ted Hughes of 28 March 1994, which is in my *Selected Letters*. It was a reply to a long letter Ted Hughes wrote me on 19 March 1994 which appeared in *Letters of Ted Hughes* (selected and edited by Christopher Reid, Faber & Faber, 2007). Hughes was Poet Laureate at the time, and I discussed the Poet Laureate's role with him:

> Traditionally the Archbishop of Canterbury provided the context of the Fire or Light for the monarch which makes possible the divine right of kings. The present incumbent at Canterbury, I am reliably informed by a friend of the woman who designed it, did not understand why his enthronement robe showed flames of Fire. (The designer knew of *The Fire and the Stones*.)
>
> Where is the true poet in relation to the procession? The Church

no longer fulfils its traditional function and so needs to be prompted by the true poet, who like Dante is actually positioned higher than the Archbishop in relation to Reality, for in his high dream (which he receives in obscurity and isolation) he has the vision and passes it on, as did Dante (the sempiternal rose, the Light of Glory). When a civilisation is still growing, the poet and Church co-exist in harmony, the one reinforcing the other as did Dante. When the parabola turns down and the civilisation declines into secularization and materialism, the Church goes with it, *but the true poet's vision remains constant, the poet stands firm*; apart, calling the monarch and the people to adhere to the vision of the civilisation's central idea, as Yeats and Eliot did to some extent. The Church has become materialistic and secularized, and being apart, the poet becomes Universalist (see stage 44 in *The Fire and the Stones*, which today reflects our new identity in the European Union, the advent of which I first predicted in 1967).

Most poets are not true poets; they are not inspired "*rsis*", and the high vision is not to be found in their work. In each generation the true poets need to find their way to the front so that they can endeavour to offer to the people the direction the Church traditionally provided. They're fighting a losing battle because the civilisation is in progressive decline and is therefore continually moving further away from its central idea which it is less and less interested in, but in each generation if a few can get the message across they hold the line and temporarily arrest further decline.

The true poet is therefore a fairly unwelcome presence at the coronation, as he offers his Holy Water and points to the light in the basket from which the Archbishop derives his authority and which he prefers to ignore. I would say your role as Poet Laureate is to ignore the Archbishop and represent the civilisation's central idea to the monarch, and to embody Reality. To interpret the role in purely social-rational terms would be a dereliction of duty in relation to your sacred office; just as, for all his wit, polish and good humour, being a great entertainer like Betjeman and striking a poetic echo with the masses was, for all its entertaining popularisation, a dereliction of duty in relation to the sacred office. I can see the role you can perform very clearly.

I said something similar in an earlier letter to Christopher Ricks of 4 May 1991, which is also in my *Selected Letters*:

> I thought you might be interested in the change in the role of the poet which the Metaphysical Revolution seeks to bring about. The poet is no longer a marginal or peripheral entertainer. As the metaphysical poet renews the vision of the Fire which is crucial to our civilisation's renewal and survival (see *The Fire and the Stones*), he is once again a central figure. The Metaphysical Revolution brings a new importance to the writing of poetry so long as it keeps society in touch with its central vision.

So in such a crisis for the European civilisation as the departure of the UK from the coming United States of Europe the role of the true poet is to keep the European civilisation in touch with its central vision of the Fire or Light and to tell the truth to imperfect politicians without being locked up in the Tower of London like the first Metaphysical poet, Sir Walter Raleigh, who wrote his *History of the World* during his thirteen years of incarceration in three rooms in the Bloody Tower, and without being banished beyond the civilised world like Ovid.

In *The Dream of Europa* (2015) I showed a united Europe celebrating 70 years of peace within the European civilisation and a fractious UK representative being told off by Churchill, who called for a United States of Europe in Zurich in 1946. What this UK representative said anticipated Brexit. In *King Charles the Wise* I wrote about the UK's post-Brexit global role outside an increasingly integrated European Union. (The UK is still, and will always continue to be, within the European civilisation.) And now in *Fools' Paradise* I write about the UK's departure from Europe (while remaining within the European civilisation), and look forward to the unification of all extant civilisations in a democratic World State that will reconcile all the world's conflicts, including the conflict between Leave and Remain. In doing this I revert to the traditional role of the true poet who is a central, not a marginal or peripheral, figure who keeps society in touch with its central vision and points the way – calls on the UK to go forward from its reasserting of national independence to participating in a global democracy.

In all times the true European poet reflects the central idea of the European civilisation as did Dante, Goethe, Milton and Eliot, but in the present time secularised readers who do not know the Fire or Light may not recognise or understand the truth of his vision. It is a fact of life that the true Metaphysical poet is today scarcely recognised within a civilisation that has lost contact with and ceased to recognise its own metaphysical central idea, and therefore may not be welcome at State events.

My Universalism

But I am above all a Universalist poet. Universalism focuses on humankind's position in the whole universe and sees all disciplines as interconnected wholes. I reflect the unity of the universe that is expressed in its literary, philosophical, historical, mystical, religious, political (in the sense of 'international politics and statecraft') and cultural disciplines – and reconcile the conflicting sides of all dialectical arguments. In this respect I understand the mind-set of Zeus, the reconciler of all, who as I show in *King Charles the Wise* wants a World State – see my *World State* and *World Constitution* (both 2018) – and who appears again in this work. As an artist I identify with all conflict, but like a good Universalist I am aware of the bigger picture beyond conflicts, the reconciling context of a coming World State.

I have a bust of Apollo at the foot of the spiral staircase to my study here at Connaught House – Apollo is the god of the Light who inspires holistic poems in structured form and metre as opposed to the raw energy and free verse inspired by Dionysus – and I am now seeking a complementary bust or statue of Zeus to place on the balcony outside my window to remind me that my overriding concern in my contemplation of the universe and the role of Brexit is to reconcile all conflicting points of view and opposites in an underlying unity, in the true Universalist manner.

27 August, 9–14 September, 3 October 2018;
3–4, 17 January, 1, 5, 15–16 April, 3, 9 May 2019

Stultifera Nauis.

Narragonice pfectionis nunqͥ

satis laudata Nauis: per Sebaſtianū Brant:vernaculo vul=
gariq̑ sermone & rhythmo ᵱ cūctoᵹ mortalium fatuitatis
semitas effugere cupiētiū directione/ speculo /cōmodoq̑ &
salute : proq̑ inertis ignaueq̑ ſtulticiͤ ppetua infamia/ exe=
cratione/& confutatione /nuᵱ fabricata : Atq̑ iampridem
per Iacobum Locher/cognométo Philomuſum:Sueuū:in
latinū traducta eloquiū : & per Sebaſtianū Brant : denuo
seduloq̑ reuiſa:foelici exorditur principio.
.1497.

Nihil sine causa.
Io.de Olpe

A page from the 1497 Latin version (by Jakob Locher) of Sebastian
Brant's German poem *Ship of Fools* (*Das Narrenschiff*), first published in
Basel, Switzerland in 1494, showing a woodcut thought to be by Albrecht
Dürer which appears on the front cover of *Fools' Paradise* (see p.ix for an
explanation of the Latin words). The text beneath begins with 'Narragonia',
the 'fools' paradise' which did not exist, to which the ship was sailing.

The Ship of Fools Bids Farewell to Europe

The same woodcut as on facing page in a later English version with a caption in English that weirdly seems to anticipate Brexit: 'The Ship of Fools Bids Farewell to Europe'

Canto I
Chequers Proposal

Sing, Muse, of harmony and nation-states
That joined a Union to progress from hates
Into one integrated region's law,
A United States of Europe free from war
Like the US, a visionary EU
Halfway to a federal World State, a new
World order and a *Pax Universalis*,
A paradise on earth, harmonious bliss;
And sing of one curmudgeonly rebel
10   That longed to break away into a Hell
Of controlling its borders, laws and gold
As once its seafaring empire of old
Traded with colonies and ruled the waves,
Still dreams of new greatness among old graves.
And sing of Zeus, now driven to despair
By the antics and dithering, now glare
Of its politicians who have misjudged
The way the world's going, who've stormed and fudged.
    Lolling in Mount Olympus's boardroom
20   Amid screens like an Emperor in gloom,
Exasperated, Zeus, at his wits' end,
Asked, "What on earth will make the British bend?"
He knows the agreement offered in March
By the EU to the UK, an arch
Through which negotiations could begin,
Was unacceptable – "toxic", "ruin" –
And as trade and technology can't keep
The Irish border in its present sleep
There must be a 'backstop': Northern Ireland will
30   Remain in the customs union and single
Market – in the EU – with a border
Down the Irish Sea. The UK would prefer
The whole of the UK to remain set

In the customs union and single market.
He knows the UK's choice: accept EU
Law or forever split the Union in two.
He knows that Davis's White Paper, known
As Canada plus-plus, the best of Canada's own
Deal plus the best South Korea and Japan
40   Agreed plus services, a 'mixed-salad' plan,
Was quickly rejected by the EU,
Which looked for a less confrontational view.
He knows the European Council's wise
And's said, "There's a deal if there's compromise,
If both sides move their red lines secretly
And take their leaders with them gradually."
Although the Council's not the Commission
And Barnier, it speaks for the twenty-seven.
He knows the UK's always practised cool
50   *Divide et impera*, 'divide and rule'
Or 'divide and conquer', to control events,
Smash concentrations of power to fragments
That have less power to implement hostile
Strategy, pacify by treacherous guile.
     Pragmatic Zeus will settle for a pact
That keeps his goal of a World State intact.
He's sent Hermes, his messenger, to scout.
"One way to get the Brexiteers out,"
Hermes reported, "is to encourage May's
60   Own adviser Robbins to reappraise
Brexit and lay before the Cabinet
A compromise plan that will cause much fret
Among key Brexiteers, who may resign.
The plan will cause the rest to realign
With what Olympus wants, a strong EU.
I have put this in hand. I've found it's true
That voters were misled: promised payments
To the NHS and no immigrants.
A poster showed a queue to leave Syria,

70   Voters were told they're coming to Dover.
We want a UK-EU compromise,
A deal that will come as a big surprise.
Ahead of that, for public consumption
We want a straight choice that will embolden –
Call for a second referendum on
'No deal' or staying in so Brexit's gone.
     "I've been working on how to achieve this
Through the press and TV – and artifice.
We want the man who wrote *King Charles the Wise*
80   And *World State* as he has perceptive eyes.
He has been given a jar of 'Zeus honey',
Manna he's had with his breakfast muesli,
Spiritual nourishment like the Eucharist
That imparts our gods' knowledge like a mist
That envelops the brains of mere mortals
And opens minds to Light with its herbals –
His PA brought it back from Zakynthos
As a gift, prompted by me, for her boss –
And so he's now blessed with divine foresight
90   Like Tiresias and is inspired to write
Whatever you would like, he'll point the way
Forward in this chaos, do what we say
In the tradition of Dryden and Pope.
He'll see the future as a time of hope.
I caught him by his bust of Apollo.
He sees into what the EU can grow."
     And so your poet, cornered by Hermes,
In his daily obeisance, at ease,
Gazing at Apollo's unseeing eyes,
100   Heard from behind, "Zeus knows that you are wise,
You already know what you have to do,
Olympus and Apollo count on you
To tell the truth about the Brexit squeeze,"
And scented Zeus's Paradise in the breeze
And, turning, saw no one in the warm air,

And knew his task, to heal national despair;
While on Olympus, bent before a screen,
Zeus studies Chequers' Great Hall, where grown men preen.

Chequers in deep Buckinghamshire countryside,
110   Prime Ministers' retreat and Tudor pride.
A heat haze shimmers the surrounding fields
As a desert mirage conceals and shields
An illusion that there's a lake ahead.
Heat waves disclose a Cabinet misled,
Sitting round a table on the terrace, each face
In white shirts, in their distant hiding-place.
       And now inside, no phones and sweltering,
A manor-house, no air-conditioning,
After coffee, chatting in the Great Hall,
120   Crammed into the tiny Hawtrey Room, all
Listening; May stands in imperial purple
And sets out Robbins' compromise jumble:
A White Paper held back so few had seen
Details she unveils for all to glean,
The red lines in her speeches and concern
In London, Florence and Munich – 'return
Control of laws, borders, money' (three bombs),
'Exit from single market and customs
Union without destroying jobs for pay
130   Or breaking up the Unionists' UK' –
Have all gone. The European Council
Had said it will move red lines if she will
Move hers, and that is what Robbins has done
In this White Paper described to Merkel, now spun:
A free-trade area with the EU
For goods but not services – that's new –
And a common EU rule book for food,
Farming and fishing and also a crude
'Facilitated Customs Agreement'
140   To remove customs checks (not yet current),

And final say on courts and laws, and now
Collective responsibility – ow! –
For *all* the Cabinet, and in the hall
Taxi cards for all who resign. Some gall
To take away their ministerial cars
At once if their manifesto-based view jars –
"If you resign you'll be replaced and then
You will immediately be forgotten" –
Especially as the taxi firm has ceased
150   Trading and resigners must trudge at least
A mile through heat to the road. No walk-outs
To May's relief. A buffet lunch and doubts.
It looks an EU treaty, written by
Barnier, with Robbins conceding like an ally.
Just as a Headmistress presents to her staff
A new policy, and all tense and do not laugh,
So May's presented to her Cabinet
A new policy that is now a threat.
      Then four hours in the Grand Parlour to agree
160   A soft deal on customs and trade, a plea
To the EU to compromise as well
In a halfway house that few will now sell.
Davis says he disagrees with the plan,
The EU'd want more concessions – and ban.
The Chequers plan means stay in the EU
Without a vote, half-in, half-out, and through.
In a six-minute moan on how hard it
Will be to sell to the country, misfit
Johnson calls the plan a turd and avers
170   It's a polished turd, there are polishers –
Civil servants like Robbins. But his joint-
Leaver Gove backs the plan, a turning-point.
Now Johnson toasts the plan in syrup words,
So much more pleasant than his foul-mouthed turds.
      The biggest meeting of May's premiership
Has shocked and troubled but she's kept her grip.

Though a type-one diabetic, she's stayed
Calm and in charge, a reconciling maid.
Dinner, and now there's no more argument,
180   After twelve hours of heat all are now bent.
Before the ministers' phones are returned
Downing Street makes a news statement. Concerned
Voters for Leave detect a huge sell-out.
There's uproar on the air waves, pundits pout.
    Now it's revealed that May had sold her plan
To Merkel in Berlin before this clan
Came to hear this overture to Europe,
This attempt to unblock the EU's 'Stop'.
The Commission's Riso the previous day
190   Showed slides to EU Ambassadors that say
The UK'd gain an advantage by staying
In the single market only for trading
Goods (which May informed Merkel she wants). Although
The EU kept this quiet to keep May's show
In power as they would rather deal with May
Than hard-line Brexiteers. After the UK
Lobbied, this slide-show arrived at Chequers
In time for May's briefing of her ministers.
Johnson's toasted the plan in a U-turn –
200   Ironic or unprincipled, or gurn?
He'd said the UK'd be a vassal state
Under the EU's rules, a dreadful fate.
Some say she has appeased the behemoth,
This agreement between two wings is froth,
She's vacillated and now compromised
And sold out the voters, and is despised.
As a deer eyes pastures beyond a wire fence
And cannot enter but won't leave and, tense,
Loiters, dithers, wanting to be in the view,
210   So May frequented the margins of the EU.

All pragmatists see the facts as they are,

All ideologues live a dream from afar.
They dream global Britain will do much trade –
With the non-EU world – that will not fade,
Live in ever-growing prosperity
And scorn all compromise as too costly.
The Brexiteers live in a fools' paradise
That's undeliverable like unmelting ice.
Hard-line Brexiteers hate the soft Brexit
220   Of the Chequers plan, which, they say, will hit
The UK hard by making rule-takers
Without influence in place of rule-shapers.
     Yet the Cabinet backs a middle way.
Aren't they, too, foolish in believing they
Can win the agreement of the EU
To a halfway fudge when the EU's view
Is that *they* didn't leave and need not budge
From the four freedoms an ECJ judge
Will defend beside the single market
230   And customs union – why should *they* fret?
Cabinet middle-wayers are middling nice,
But they too live in a fools' paradise.
What kind of Brexit did voters vote for?
Brexiteers did not say, no one knows or
Has any idea if it's EEA,
Canada plus or plus-plus or Norway,
Customs union, single market, border
With Southern Ireland or – so much clearer –
The Irish Sea, or 'facilitated'
240   Technology – a border in the head
Till someone invents the technology.
Like the Ship of Fools we are all at sea.
May's capitulation to a small band
Of ideologues who do not understand
And can't articulate why leaving's good
For UK's sovereignty and brotherhood,
Has confected an appeasement no one

Thinks the EU will accept; rather shun.

The wise medievals' great Ship of State
250   Was sailed by fools – a Ship of Fools all hate.
In Plato's *Republic* book six we see
A ship, a deaf, part-blind captain who's key
With little knowledge of navigating,
Sailors who quarrel about the steering
Though none have been taught skills. All want to steer
And kill or throw overboard all they hear
Are preferred, make the captain drunk and trip,
Then mutiny and take over the ship
And eat and drink the stores and then promote
260   All who were mutineers and seized the boat,
And they abuse the rest. The true pilot
Who's attuned to the year and seasons (hot
And cold), sky, stars, winds and must be steerer
They call a good-for-nothing star-gazer.
     Beyond this Cornish window and the quay
An old sailing-ship tosses on the sea.
It could be from the 1494
Basel woodcut Ship of Fools, some of whom wore
Jester's hats. All were sailing to arrive
270   In paradise, that could be reached, alive,
In Narragonia – a legendary
Wonderful, fool-inhabited country –
Beyond the waves by sailing with a crew
Of fools who ran the ship without a clue.

Canto II
Brexiteers Resign

Sing, Muse, of the consequences of the plot
To split the Brexiteers and curb the lot
So Zeus's plan for a World State would rule
(Via the EU) both wise man and the fool –
The populists and nationalists who dream
And promise an undeliverable scheme.
 A long weekend of disquiet and anger
Within the party and country, dogma
Has been breached, grass-roots activists lament
10 A soft Brexit, there is open dissent
From May's own constituency chairman:
One more such move and she will be fallen.
Her red line has been crossed, Leavers who bayed
In the referendum have been betrayed.
MPs' no-confidence letters will be
With the 1922 Committee.
Forty-eight will trigger a leadership
Contest beyond the grip of the Chief Whip.
May's pleased she's united her Cabinet,
20 Though shocked at the Brexit Secretary's threat
To resign as he can't support her fudge.
He's close to leaving, he just needs a nudge.
The EU rejected *his* White Paper,
And May's replaced it with Robbins' "monster".
 On Sunday Davis muses, can't decide.
He does a decision tree, now his guide.
(It explores outcomes and scenarios
By using branching methods that disclose.)
He sits at his desk and puts in the aim:
30 Frictionless trade, Northern Ireland the same –
No border; no alignment with EU
Regulations, EU to share this view.
EU manufacturers' urging the EC

Won't be enough, so the UK must agree
To walk away to 'no deal' to persuade
The EU to accept the UK's trade.
So the UK must prepare for a 'no deal',
But dwelling on disruption won't appeal
And undermines the threat as self-harming
And there won't be a Commons supporting
Majority. Now the decision tree
Has led to a dead end. Davis can see
Brexit can go nowhere, he must resign,
Jump ship so he's not blamed in a public whine
For offering false hopes and for raising
Expectations, for falsely promising.
His brief has been replaced by Robbins' powers,
He's only met Barnier for just seven hours
In the last six months, he has in effect
Been superseded, and he has now checked:
The Chequers proposal doesn't contain
The referendum's spirit, that is plain.
    He's told May her plan is unworkable,
He knows the EU'll reject and grumble.
He sees May and her Chief Whip, says he'll quit
In the national interest, he can't commit
To supporting her illusory plan –
A principled decision by one man.
His letter says he can't deliver on
The referendum's mandate, which has gone;
And the supposed control by Parliament
Will be illusory, in his judgement.
Now his deputy follows. Consensus
Has broken down, May's shocked and dubious.
But Robbins' plan is working, *he* was key.
Hermes tells Zeus, who rubs his hands in glee.

Monday morning, and May makes Raab the new
Brexit Secretary. His different view

40

50

60

Is that 'no deal' is likely and he should
70   Explain it so it's seen a deal is good.
      Now there is pressure on Johnson to leave:
Does he wear his principles on his sleeve?
At Chequers he congratulated May
For securing a Cabinet OK
But would not sign a joint article, seal
With Hammond support for the Chequers deal.
Has he waved a white flag at the sell-out?
Has he bottled his chance in a new bout
Of leadership challenge? Is he more like
80   Appeaser Chamberlain than Churchillian tyke?
Davis can challenge May. And should not he,
Too, resign to challenge in 'Look at me'?
Johnson's advisers say he should tell May
That he plans to resign later that day.
Johnson, in two minds, rings 10 Downing Street,
Which leaks the news at once, so no retreat.
Davis is told during an interview,
Is sad: Johnson "didn't have to go too".
Just as a squirrel hangs upside down by its tail
90   And rattles nuts in a bird feeder's jail
But can't get access and stares disconsolate,
So Johnson stared at goodies he'd found too late.
      In gloom Johnson writes his letter, racked with doubt:
The UK is not fully heading out
But for 'semi-Brexit', a colony
Of Brussels, and the dream of Leave – to be
In control of our democracy – is
Dying, suffocated by self-doubt (not his).
May icily replies she is surprised
100   And defends the proposal he's despised.
At the FO his staff now drink champagne.
No more gaffes and blunders, order can reign.
He won't move out of Carlton Gardens for
Another three weeks, his gloom is too raw.

(And his wife's thrown him out for an affair
With an aide and he has to find somewhere
To live in London, or he must retire
Back to his second home in Oxfordshire.)
He sits around in his pants in the heat
110 • And broods that his choice led to a defeat.
Just as a toad puffs up to vaunt its worth
And then deflates back to its former girth,
So Johnson subsided into croaky calm
And squatted in depression far from harm.
So once again a Brexiteer's fate
Involves a fleeing from the Ship of State.
Johnson's idea was never going to work.
Shocked Leave won the referendum, part-Turk,
He's got out before he's blamed for the mess.
120 Is he personally accountable? Yes.
    But so was Cameron, who had no plan
For Brexit and should not have called a clan
Referendum to unite his party
And risk impoverishing the country.
Johnson – and Farage and Gove – loosely warned
That seventy-seven million Turks all scorned
Might head for the UK, which was believed
By low-IQ voters, who were deceived.
Aren't the Brexiteers and Cameron to blame
130 In equal measure for the UK's shame?
Now Robbins smirks, having devised the trap
Of joint articles to make Johnson snap;
And on Olympus Zeus is delighted.
The two main Brexiteers are as stone-dead.

Half an hour after news of Johnson's fall
May stands at the dispatch-box as each call
By the Speaker brings hostile questions from
Leavers and Remainers, each like a bomb.
Two ministers resigned within a day,

140 She's ambushed from both sides: the Leavers say
   'The Chequers deal keeps the UK within
   Parts of the single market – in the bin.'
   Remainers say, 'Back the customs union.'
   All jeer and heckle 'Betrayal' and 'Con'.
     And in Brussels EU officials gloat,
   Mock "the flight of the Brexiteers" and the vote
   In the referendum. "It's all a mess,
   Now they're leaving for higher ground, we guess
   The rats are fleeing from a sinking ship.

150 They've created," Tusk says with a curled lip,
   "The biggest problem in UK-EU
   Relations." Juncker is sarcastic too,
   Praises the unity of the Cabinet.
   One says, "The blueprint's flawed at the outset.
   Its customs proposal is untested."
   The EU's ready to declare it dead.
     May is assailed on three fronts: Tory right,
   Remainers and Brussels. She lowers her sight
   And does not look at her Commons critics.

160 Then at the 1922, more kicks.
   Thirty-eight no-confidence letters received.
   Two more ministers have resigned, are grieved.
   But she will soldier on and the EU
   Will back her as "least worst", close to their view.
   There's no Parliamentary majority
   For a hard or soft Brexit, which means she
   Will crash out with no deal, WTO.
   She is emotional, and cried to know
   That Duncan Smith will vote against the plan

170 And will oppose her like a straight Roman.
     Next day Raab speaks about the White Paper
   Before MPs' copies reach the chamber.
   A copy's in the Commons library
   And more copies are in the Press Gallery.
   There is uproar, the House is suspended.

Piles are brought in and flung about each head
For MPs to catch, and clutch, and first read.
There's chaos, Raab's not grasped their greatest need.
He's not thought the written word will compel,
His grasp of such detail does not bode well.
  It looks as if May's proposal's on ice,
Illusory and a fools' paradise.
Zeus, bent before his screen, is satisfied.
Davis and Johnson have both been denied.
Both have given up, having reached a dead end.
The EU is united, will ascend.

180

The Athenian democracy each year
Held an election in which, without fear,
All voted to banish or ostracise
The most unpopular and most unwise
Politician for the coming year. Bring
Ostrakoi, potsherds used for balloting,
So all UK citizens can reckon
And write the name of the politician
Who's been a fool and most deserves his fate –
Has done the most disservice to the State –
Of being banished and exiled beyond
The UK borders as a vagabond
For messing up the public weal, and see
If the name begins with a J or D.
  In the fifteenth-century *Ship of Fools*, a tale
By Brant published in Basel, a ship sets sail
Bound for paradise, Narragonia,
Where St Grobian's patron saint of vulgar
And coarse people, a ship laden with fools
Who steer as they think best, free from all rules.
All the follies and vices of their time
Are in this shipload of nitwits and grime.
The Ship of State is like the Ship of Fools,
It too's sailed by a captain and crew with rules

190

200

210

Who bypass rocks, wind in their sails, and toss
And bob on the sparkling waves and criss-cross,
And on the decks stand the public all bound
For a destination, hoping they're not drowned,
Believing they're heading for a Utopia
Their Government has found, a provider,
A paradise where they'll land and be free
Like settlers in the New World's territory.

Canto III
Trump's Visit

Sing, Muse, of how the US President
Castigated the Chequers agreement
Which had already split the Tory right
And dispatched two ministers into night.
Sing how the President, with limited
Understanding, blundered in and, knucklehead,
Unwitting ally of Zeus and the EU,
Blurted his opposition to the new
Chequers deal that the EU did not rate.
10   Zeus loathed 'America First' with pure hate
As it was divisive for humankind
And banned Muslims and Mexicans behind
A wall Trump planned. Globalist Zeus called for
No borders or walls: a world without war.
Having said the UK is "in turmoil"
And called Johnson his "friend" – made May's blood boil –
Trump has been at the NATO conference,
And lambasted members and knocked some sense
Into their heads so they've agreed to send
20   Thirty-four billion dollars more to end
Their over-reliance on the US
In blocking Russia's military success,
Incursions in Baltic states and elsewhere –
Russia who's had spies expelled for a severe
Novichok attack in a UK hit.
     Now still in Brussels before his visit
To the UK, in a *Sun* interview
He continues his combative pooh-pooh:
He says Germany's captive to Russia
30   Because it gets its energy from her,
The Nord Stream 2 pipeline for natural gas –
While the US defends German landmass;
Says May's Chequers' soft-Brexit blueprint would "kill"

Future trade deals with the US, which will
Do a deal with the EU instead, he
Advised her to sue the EU, but she
Has gone the other way and won't be free
To do deals with a non-EU country.
He said, "I thought you Brits wanted Brexit."
40   He means that the PM's vision of it
Is not what UK voters voted for.
The Chequers deal has caused a civil war.
It's been a humiliation for May,
It blows her reassurances away.

Blenheim Palace, Churchill's birthplace, echo
Of war with Germany and Europe's slow
Growth to a United States of Europe
For which Churchill called at Zurich. Now stop –
By helicopter in black tie, Trump lands
50   At twilight and is greeted by massed bands
And a parade, bagpipes. And then, grasping
May's hand, he leads her up the steps, holding
On to balance, and goes in to dinner:
Salmon and beef. The Duke of Marlborough
Is host to the Establishment's *noblesse*.
      Trump flies back for the night at the US
Ambassador's Winfield House. Protesters
Blow whistles, beat spoons on saucepans, faint slurs
Which don't disturb his sleep, there's no tumult.
60   Next morning, avoiding a new insult –
A floating balloon, Trump as a baby,
Eyes closed, wearing a safety-pinned nappy –
He and May fly to Sandhurst and witness
A demonstration by the SAS.

The transatlantic leaders of the Free
World, one ex-Empire, one ex-colony,
Fly in for lunch at Chequers, where crass Trump

Sits in Churchill's worn armchair, smug and plump,
And hero-worships half-American
70   Churchill who won the war, a true 'Roman'.
Outside there's a press conference in heat haze.
     Now Trump's harsh words have become lavish praise.
As a fox sidles near a chicken coop
And looks nonchalantly away mid-snoop,
So Trump looks casual as he stands by May
And lick his lips at what he's going to say.
He apologises for his diatribe
On how she had killed their trade deal, his gibe.
The *Sun* interview's "fake news" – no, watch TV.
80   Now "Whatever you do's OK with me."
"She's doing a terrific job," he shouts.
He's rowing back, but's firm on the deal doubts.
He says, "I want a trade deal," but it's true
The Chequers plan's tied her to the EU.
It's awkward but he's held the line; he's tough,
Then soothes away the pain, he's rough, then bluff.
He's praised her but has not backtracked at all.
It doesn't mean there's a trade deal to trawl:
Impossible to trade with the US
90   If the EU accept her plan, say Yes.
     Twelve days on, the US and the EU
Reach the deal trailed in the *Sun* interview,
To avoid a trade war. Trump and Juncker
Announce it at the White House; May's plan's the spur.
     But now Trump flies to Windsor, where the Queen
Stands waiting to greet him. A pageant scene.
They inspect troops, in the Oak Room have tea.
It overruns eighteen minutes, then he
Flies off to Scotland, then to meet Putin.
100   The visit's over, May's head's in a spin.
Trump's world, in which America comes first
And no country has immigrants, is cursed.
His trade protectionism's out of date,

His tweets and blurts are uninformed and hate.
A bold leader with a world-view that's not nice,
He seems to live in a fools' paradise.
Trump's scorn's shown the UK's isolated
But within the UK the high-minded
Brexiteers' view's been strengthened, they're now bent
110   On opposing May's plan in Parliament.

O look at the crew on the Ship of State.
O see all the mariners agitate
In peaked caps like mutineers who rescind,
Aligning with a favourable wind
To be blown in the direction that all
Believe is best to achieve a landfall
On the ideal territory of their dreams
On a coast no one's been to, and that seems
Yet undiscovered, which they're sure exists
120   Just on the horizon beyond the mists.
O see the mariners, immune to shocks,
Heading for their dreamland, and submerged rocks.

Canto IV
Cabinet at War

Sing, Muse, of May's struggle with Parliament
As Leave and Remain expressed fierce intent
Without appreciating hidden goodwill
From Zeus and the European Council.
    Nine resignations to date, and MPs
Are thinking of their constituencies:
Support the Chequers plan and lose their seat,
Or block it and face electoral defeat
Which would bring ultra-left Corbyn to power.

10   Faced with Scylla and Charybdis, they cower,
Not wanting to find themselves out of work,
Salvaging their principles and each perk.
With both Rees-Mogg and Mandelson opposed
May is attacked from both sides and enclosed.
MPs from feuding wings insult and gore
Across the green benches in civil war
On the Taxation (Cross-border Trade) Bill,
And vote on amendments as if they'd kill.
Rees-Mogg's European Research Group's strong.

20   May concedes four amendments that look wrong:
There'll be no borders in the Irish Sea,
No customs union and no VAT
Regime, no taxes and duties in crates
For the EU unless it reciprocates.
She's trying to hold together both wings,
The Chequers plan seems in turmoil, she clings,
Says, "Back me or I'll call an election."
MPs wince, sensing jobcentres beckon.
    Next day in the Customs Debate, a counter-

30   Rebellion from Remain in the chamber,
She wins all the votes on the amendments
Including the customs union, assents
Made possible by four Labour MPs

Who did not vote for Corbyn; and so she's
Had a *coup* against the Brexiteers, who
Have failed in their drive against the EU
And in their attempt to derail the plan
Approved at Chequers, the compromise 'can'.

Davis has made his resignation speech
40   In measured terms that demanded a breach
With the EU. Now Johnson stands to speak,
He's brushed his hair (of sorts), statesman-like chic.
After two days dressed in pants, much depressed,
Wondering if he was too hasty, distressed.
Will his statement be like Howe's, that did for
Thatcher? No Cabinet attend, it's war,
And some MPs have folded arms and show
Body language that disapproves, a blow.
He contrasts May's old Lancaster-House speech
50   With her later fog of self-doubt or reach,
No negotiating offer to Brussels,
An exit fee and dithering, no quells
Of the ECJ and Northern Ireland.
The UK's a rule-taking vassal, EU-planned.
"It's not too late to save Brexit – it's now
Brexit in name only, a limbo." Wow?
Not really, a bit flat, no trademark jokes,
A sober speech but no detailed plan pokes
Through, "Believe in this country" is not a plan.
60   So ends his case that he is a statesman.
    He expressed Leavers' sense of betrayal,
A damning speech aimed at May by a rebel,
The dream of a Churchillian wannabe
That he believes is the reality:
An independent, more open UK,
Outward-looking and with a greater say,
More engaged with the world through trade deals, so
Global Britain as fifty years ago.

So ends two years as Foreign Secretary.
70   He made gaffes, did little and saw scarcely
Anything through, he did not even sign
A prepared document that would headline
Diplomatic immunity to the young
British-Iranian mother who was flung
In a Tehran jail and not helped – clench fists –
By his blurting she'd been training journalists.
(Nor did he deal with your poet's two works
That after six months were called lost – that irks.)
He's been called the worst Foreign Secretary
80   Since the Great War, in living memory.
He swayed the referendum with his view
But did not have a plan to see it through
And having brought the nation to distress
Left without clearing up his turd-like mess.
So two years on no one knows what's ahead
And he feels no guilt that he has misled.

At Hartwell House, where the French King and court
Lived in exile, your poet walked and sought
And found statues of Zeus and Juno through
90   An arch, either side of a lawn, and knew
Intuitively the ancient bearded god
Who looked down from twelve feet up, with a nod
Was beckoning him and preparing to speak.
He crossed the lawn, stood below his right cheek
And suddenly felt surrounded with Light
And as within a mist – it was so bright,
The radiance – he heard Zeus address his soul:
"Nicholas, all is going well. The Whole
Is one harmony, the One, as you've seen.
100   All opposites are reconciled, what's been,
Is now and is to come, a unity.
And so it is with region and country.
You know humankind needs a new World State

That will abolish war and make life great
For all 7.3 billion on the earth,
And when this comes there will be a new birth
In humankind's spiritual brotherhood.
The EU's heading forward, that is good.
The UK is a part of this process
110   And historically led the progress,
But doesn't seem to want to take part now,
Judging from the referendum mess. How
Can a united Europe integrate
And guide the UK towards a World State,
Along with the twenty-seven and with new
Members making a fifty-strong EU?
How can the UK best rejoin Europe?
How can the Brexit nightmare best develop?
Compromise deal? Second referendum?
120   Revoking Article 50? What's to come?
Please tell me how you see it, so I can
Work to support it. It's the Chequers plan?"
        Your poet answered Olympian Jove:
"Mighty Lord of the Universe, I strove
For six decades to understand our time
And I've read many papers in my prime
And have discovered the Law of History,
That the progress of civilisations is no mystery,
That each of the twenty-five rises, then falls
130   Through sixty-one stages, that a World State calls.
And I've researched Brexit and my best guess
Regarding the Chequers plan is, 'Oh yes,
It's the way forward – to keep the UK locked in
To EU rules so leaving can't begin.
It's a halfway house. Please let me explain
The politics behind *impasse* and pain.
        "The background to the Chequers agreement
Is Barnier's hard line and one salient
Detail commentators have overlooked:

140 The European Council's now unhooked
From the Commission, which is split between
Barnier, who wants a deal, and Selmayr's spleen –
He wants a damaging exit so all
The twenty-seven EU states see a fall,
That exit's dreadful, would take them downhill.
The European Council's said it will
Lift its red line on free movement to dress
A deal and allow the UK access
To the customs union and single market

150 So long as she accepts – this must be met –
EU standards on environmental,
Social and customs protections – verbal
Echoes in Johnson's resignation speech –
In perpetuity, which Johnson would screech
Would make the UK an EU vassal state.
On this model, the UK would relate
To the EU like Jersey and the Channel Isles.
This is not widely known to Anglophiles.
Jersey's only part of the EU for trade

160 In goods, otherwise it's not in the EU's shade.
It voluntarily uses EU
Laws and international standards as glue.
It's separate but is also aligned,
And like-minded. EU guile's intertwined,
It's found in last December's backstop pact,
When the UK quietly gave in and cracked
At EU demands, capitulated.
The Irish backstop can't be amended
With ambiguous words and compromise.

170 Chequers is pro-Remainer in disguise.
Chequers is a halfway house Remainers spurn,
That's aligned with the EU for a future return."

    Zeus stared down at your poet with wide eyes –
The cleverness of the plan took him by surprise –
And spoke: "Thank you, even I do not know

What's going to happen. There's free will, I'm slow
To interpret what's been going on.
I did not know some of what you said's gone.
I'm cut off from the detail of the world.
180   I see broad patterns, not how they've unfurled.
Tell me, what do you see happening next?"
      Your poet, shocked by his words and perplexed
That he was instructing Olympian Jove,
Said: "It's like scouring Europe for treasure trove,
All I can give is a considered guess.
Some of the Commission want no progress.
Some, with the Council, want the Jersey deal.
Can they sell it to their voters? I feel
They can – it means duping voters, who are
190   Less stupid than ministers think, by far.
If they can't, there'll be 'no deal', and a choice:
A second referendum and new voice:
'Do you accept no-deal and dreadful terms
Which deliver the Brexit vote with worms?'
Or 'Would you rather stay in the EU?'
Brexit's been difficult, I think it's true
They'd rather stay. But many will feel duped
The true deal's veiled, and Europe don't want it scooped.
      "There are two extreme ways in the divided UK,
200   And a middle way may not be the best way.
The best way forward is to make a choice
To stay in the EU, and retain a voice
In deciding policy. But the worst way
Is to crash out without a deal in disarray
With trade links broken down and stockpiling.
The middle way – half-in, half-out – is going
With the Chequers plan, aligning to the EU
But losing a voice and not being true
To the Good-Friday pact that made violence cease
210   In Northern Ireland. The best way keeps the peace."
As the Pythia spoke at Apollo's Oracle,

So spoke your poet in inspired babble.
    Zeus nodded and spoke: "I'm pleased that the two
Brexiteers resigned. Remain can win through."
Zeus nodded his thanks and slowly the mist
Of Light dispersed, ending your poet's tryst.
Now he looked up at a weathered, pitted
Statue as inanimate as stone, and dead.
    Next day your poet passed Chequers' chaos
220   And stopped at a farm shop and looked across
Fields at the distant Tudor hall and at
The terrace where the Cabinet all sat
That hot Friday two weeks back they first saw
The Chequers plan and launched a civil war.

On the Ship of Fools above the waves' tossing
The crew's divided into two warring
Factions that sabotage what the other's done,
Constantly change direction with the sun
So the ship zigzags as she sails, bound for
230   The paradise in the captain's mind and awe,
The blessed country of plenty that lies
Beyond the waves in the crew's inferred surmise
And in the passengers' dream as they toss
And vie to steer the ship out of chaos.
A man's thrown overboard into the brine.
A fool swigs from a leather flask of wine.
There's a brawl on the ship. Order has gone.
The crew are fighting as the ship ploughs on
Towards its paradise across the waves.
240   Passengers are alarmed, fear watery graves
As the wooden ship creaks and sways and rolls
From side to side precariously. One extols,
"Unite and steer one course, for our safety."
Now passengers maul crew to steer safely.
There is a shambles on the ship, a hate;
And there's a shambles on the Ship of State.

Canto V
European Leaders

Sing, Muse, how the EU savaged the plan,
How Barnier of the Commission began
To probe, dissect and then eviscerate
The Chequers proposal put on his plate.
    The UK signed up to an agreement
In December, and this plan's different.
He says the customs proposals are flawed,
Wrap trade in red tape and encourage fraud
And UK firms will get an unfair boost.
10   The backstop agreed in March is at roost.
Irish backstop by Friday or no deal.
There can be no cherry-picking appeal,
Having cake and eating it, or else all
EU member-states will want the same haul.
But the two resignations are welcome,
It's good they're out now before more bunkum.
    May cleared the plan with Merkel, was naïve?
Is it just a fantasy to believe
Twenty-seven EU countries will accept
20   The Chequers proposal? Has it been prepped
In a fools' paradise? Or are the fools
The Commission, for sticking to their rules?
Raab skips the first day of new Brexit talks,
Says 'no deal' is welcome: just hardball squawks.
And: "No trade deal, no cash for the EU."
    Now May has had a quiet Remainer *coup*:
She's announced the UK'll shadow (and pay)
The EU till 2020's last day,
And she's now in charge, above Raab (who'll drop),
30   The Minister for Exiting Europe,
With her mandarin Robbins now the Head
Of the Exiting Europe Unit, fed
By a hundred officials, all hungry,

With overall responsibility
For preparing and then conducting all
Negotiations; a measure of Raab's fall.
So Raab has been stripped of leading the large
EU negotiations, May's in charge;
And Barnier's said "Permanent backstop by
40   Next Friday or no deal" and May's reply
Is: "Backstop till 2020's last day,
It will cover the whole of the UK."
Merkel's said May should meet EU leaders
In Salzburg, and now May tells ministers
To tour EU capitals and progress
Her Chequers plan in the summer recess.
     Again Barnier meets Raab and both agree
There's no progress on a withdrawal treaty
With a backstop – no hard Irish border.
50   "Salzburg's pointless," Barnier says, "not a sliver
Of difference exists between all the fine
EU leaders and me. They're all in line."
The Facilitated Customs Arrangement
(The UK collects tariffs to be sent
To Brussels) is unworkable: "The EU certainly
Won't delegate its customs policy,
VAT, excise duty or rules to a non-member
State." And the thirty-nine-billion-pound, er,
'Exit fee' can't depend on a trade deal.
60   The EU won't accept much of May's *Spiel*.
Barnier seems to have vetoed and closed down
The plan by greeting key parts with a frown.
Is this a front to conceal the moving
Of red lines by both sides and the bringing
Of a deal to UK voters that can
Raise a second referendum: the plan,
Or stay in the EU? It has a feel
Of the UK's crashing out with no deal.

⌐The hot weather that heated the conflict
70   Has now quietened it down, the calm's perfect.
MPs have gone off to the countryside
Where cows rest in shade, carp are still, birds glide.
All Europe sweats in the sweltering sun,
And politicians fan themselves, half-done.

      In Salzburg May takes her Chequers planning
To the Austrian Chancellor, Kurz, hoping
To prise pragmatic member-states who'll trade
With the UK from the Commission's shade,
Blatantly bypass it, rein Barnier in.
80   Kurz says, "I'm loyal to the EU" – that's spin –
"And crashing out will hurt you more than us,
Negotiations have gone without fuss,
I hope we can avoid a hard Brexit."
He'll support Brexit talks at the summit
In Salzburg in September in a helpful way
When EU leaders could ask Barnier
For concessions to the UK to seal
A good Norway-style – or Jersey-style – deal.
The Czech Republic's Prime Minister waits,
90   He says the bloc of EU member-states
Is united behind Barnier. May stirs
Up Estonian and Portuguese leaders.
Barnier warns, "Don't try to circumnavigate
Me, I speak for each EU nation-state."

      Is her tour to detach EU leaders
Folly? Has she, one of the Remainers,
Been sucked into argumentative advice
And's now of the Brexit fools' paradise?
Or is this 'detaching' a front to hide
100   Negotiations on red lines each side
And a Jersey or Channel-Islands deal?
A poll reports a shift in what all feel,
Most polled want a second referendum.

      Then May and Kurz attend, both looking glum,

Mozart's *The Magic Flute*. Can May commune
With a magic flute that trills a Jersey tune:
In the EU for trade, closely aligned,
But separate despite her friendly mind?
A blood-moon eclipse, this night the moon's in
110   Earth's shadow, doom-mongers warn of ruin,
A once-in-a-lifetime event – Brexit? –
And the end of the world's impending split.

May goes to Lake Garda on holiday
But leaves to meet Macron near Saint-Tropez
At Fort de Brégançon on an islet
Off the Côte d'Azure, seventeenth-century pet
Retreat of Napoleon and Presidents.
    They sit in shade, each with three assistants.
Macron wants more integration and's shocked.
120   The UK's been a barrier and should be blocked.
The EU is looking to integrate
As it progresses towards a World State.
She shows Macron how her red lines have moved
As the European Council approved
And asks him to bypass Barnier's genteel
"*Non*" on customs: Chequers deal or 'no deal'.
She says she's accepted "a common rule
Book" of EU regulation, a pool,
That's cost two ministers. He says with pep:
130   "I must stress that there cannot be a step-
By-step 'having your cake and eating it'."
The EU's on its guard for any split.
A cake-and-eat-it Brexit was a great
Illusion that bequeathed a messy state.
And there must now be an Irish backstop.
There cannot be new problems for Europe.
Like a faithful dog attached to his master's way
Macron has stayed loyal to Barnier.
    France cannot accept the Chequers dogma:

140   A flow of goods, open Irish border,
UK controls on Europeans' movement.
Preserving the EU trumps all intent
To get close to the UK – no romance.
The EU states must keep their hard-line stance.
He is with Barnier who has warned at press
Briefings by the Commission on progress
That Brussels cannot and will not accept
The customs measures in what May has prepped.
There's no press conference – to show his support
150   For the Commission, or, within the Fort
To preserve the Jersey plan's secrecy
In a verbal fort from publicity?
    Back in the UK there is a silence
Over the meeting and a general sense
The EU must punish the UK, cleave,
So EU states like Italy won't leave.
Has Macron said, "Have a second 'Dublin'
Referendum on 'no deal' or 'stay in'"?
Will there be endless meetings and delay
160   In the European Council's headway
Until the UK public can succumb,
Vote Remain in a new referendum?
May's seen the EU leaders, we're perplexed.
There's a loud silence, what will happen next?

A shock! A grating, shuddering blow. Ring
The bell, sound the alarm. The zigzagging
Ship of State's heading on to rocks. The voyage
Will end in disaster, on a submerged ridge.
Where is the destination described so
170   Confidently by a captain and crew aglow?
Where is the dream Utopia, where's the trail
To the paradise to which all set sail
So trustingly before the crew fell out
And mutinied, wanting to steer and shout?

Canto VI
UK Prepares for 'No Deal'

Sing, Muse, of the ruin if there's no deal,
Of the collapse of the dream and all heal
That leaving the EU'd leave the UK
Better off, not worse off, a hope that's fey,
A fantasy like never-melting ice;
An illusion of the fools' paradise
That rebooting UK politics will
Reconcile liberalism and soft-shrill
Nationalism and globalisation and expand
10   Democratic self-government as a brand
With openness to all and, requisite,
A buccaneering commercial spirit,
Migrant communities integrated,
Discontent neutered; so the UK's well-led,
Controlling its borders and destiny
Like Switzerland or Australia, set free,
Pro-capitalist, open to talent (famed)
And foreign capital, its *élite* tamed,
Ordinary people's problems addressed, wise
20   After trust-breaking recessions and lies –
With a fresh start tackling hates the public's brayed:
Softness in crime, excessive foreign aid,
Costly HS2, human rights rulings
And dishonest immigration curbings.
    How different is the harsh reality
Under WTO rules: misery
If there's 'no deal' by the end of November,
Northern Ireland will have a hard border,
The UK may lose Northern Ireland. New
30   Tariffs loom, fifty-four trade deals the EU
Negotiated for its member-states
Must be renegotiated (and rates)
With numerous countries before Brexit,

But these will take several years to permit.
New York's taking business from the City,
Which will lose its established primacy.
Services, which supply eighty per cent
Of the UK's income, may now be spent.
Businesses and banks will soon relocate.
40 Airliners will be grounded, and all freight,
As they'll lose their authorisations file.
Heathrow'll be shut for two months, quite a while.
Goods will cost more, the price of food will rise.
Queues of cars and lorries will stretch and surprise
For hundreds of miles in North France, and in
The UK, for at least four years, within
Two Kent motorways and Manston airfield
That's linked to Dover by a narrow shield,
A dual part-single carriageway that contains
50 Twelve roundabouts within its meagre lanes.
The Army's on stand-by to deliver food
And ferry stocks, there's no space to seclude
And stockpile food in Dover. The UK
Will not export or import meat and may
Have to adopt US regulation
That won't exclude mad-cow disease – have none.
Road hauliers won't be able to carry
Goods on the Continent and are panicky.
There'll be a shortage of food and cancer drugs;
60 A bit like a medieval siege, one shrugs.
It's said that manufacturing will be
Eliminated from the economy.
The UK'll have to sell arms that'll hurt the poor,
To undesirable states making war.
Brexiteers will say, "You're trying to make
'No deal' look very bad, a great mistake.
It's Project Fear." No, Project Reality.
Eighty-four technical notices will be
Signed off by the UK on what to do

70 If 'no deal' in farming and fishing's due,
Customs and stockpiling: contingency.
  Men will look at Cameron and say he
Showed lack of statesmanship, no substantive
Politician walks away. What a div.
He gave a fifty-per-cent binary choice
Instead of a sixty-five-per-cent voice.
He knew that some would protest-vote to cease
Austerity and cuts and 'no pay increase',
Not vote on Europe – the statutory task.

80 The question to voters on deals should ask
"Do you want this 'no deal' or poor deal or
Do you want to stay in the EU?" – for
A second referendum in all but name.
  If the UK leaves the EU and its aim
Of trade deals with the US, India, China
Proves a fantasy and the UK's poorer,
There's food and medicine shortage and job cuts
With cheese going off in small dockside huts
And civil unrest, Brexit will be seen

90 As a catastrophe. But the verdict on screen –
When judging experts finally concur
On whether Brexit was a disaster,
On the most important crisis since the war –
May not be known for fifty years or more.
  The first Brexit was when the UK broke
With Rome, but not with Catholicism, spoke
In protest at the Roman Church's costly
Corruption and distant authority
And for a free English Catholic Church.

100 The English Reformation was a lurch
To self-governing Protestant virtue –
Not unlike the Brexit from the EU,
But then it did not leave England poorer.
  The second Brexit's a severe rupture.
Expectations have been raised, a pledge resounds.

The three hundred and fifty million pounds
To the NHS and wage increasings
Cannot be funded from Brexit savings –
The reverse, the cost of Brexit will see
110   An outflow of funds – and austerity
Will have to continue, disguised in cuts
To jobs and services, there are no gluts
Of additional money. So greater
Poverty is ahead. What will occur?
     What is about to happen? A good deal
Accepted by December will repeal
'No deal', but a referendum on its spin
May result in no Brexit, staying in,
And the Canada-style trade agreement
120   The Brexiteers want will be seen to present
A fantasy. There'll be no leadership
Or early general election to strip
May of her position as the captain
Of the Ship of State that will soon be sailing in.
     As at the time of the Suez crisis, so
The UK's divided, one half gung-ho
To leave, the other half alarmed, bemused
At the shambles. Industries are confused.
Hunt, touring Europe, says that a 'no deal'
130   Would be a mistake that all would regret, feel
For generations, a messy divorce
Should be avoided at all costs of course.
Killing the Chequers "proposal" would harm
The EU, it's a framework that can calm,
In which all problems can be shown and faced,
On which the ultimate deal will be based.
Brexiteers say, "Do not lock the UK
In orbit round the EU with no say."
Out there in the green British countryside
140   Many think Brexit will bring far and wide
Severe economic costs and that damage

Limitation should span talks like a bridge.
    The UK's sailed into disaster. Sigh,
British hubris may again be followed by
Suez-like humiliation at sea.
Will two years of pursuing a fantasy,
A fools' paradise, end back at the start
In a return to the EU's warm heart,
After wasted money and bad feeling,
150   And punitive terms and lost world standing,
Lost Thatcher rebate, lost Major opt-out,
The nation's reputation sunk? Will this rout
Be the outcome of the Salzburg summit?
Now there's a shock: May can't debate at it.
The EU's banned all UK oratory
When the twenty-seven next meet to parley.

Now Raab announces the first twenty-five
Technical notices that jolt and rive,
Credit cards will have charges, there are shrieks.
160   Medicines should be stockpiled for six weeks.
Many will be without medication.
Expats now may not receive their pension.
There will be new customs duties on made-
In-EU imports, businesses that trade
With the EU should alter their supply
Chains or call a freight-forward company
To handle new customs papers. There'll be
Hundreds of Portaloos on the M20
For gridlocked queuing lorry drivers. Yes,
170   His subtext is: 'Be reassured, unless
You're an EU official – if so, fear.'
But this won't terrify the French, who are clear.
(Perhaps he'll terrify rebel MPs
Into voting for Chequers, despite unease.)
Rompuy says 'no deal' may break the UK.
Both Scotland and Northern Ireland may stray.

The United Kingdom would turn federal –
Unions decline to federation's grumble
Like the Soviet Union's states breaking free –
180   And put Gibraltar at Madrid's mercy.
Some ministers greet Raab's words with a subdued jeer.
Hammond complains the UK will lose near
Nine per cent of its GDP if no
Deal, and by 2033 borrow
Eighty billion pounds just to make ends meet.
He's undermined Raab with talk of defeat.
Leaving the EU without a treaty
Will send a shock through the economy.
As a parakeet clings to a cage with its bill
190   And grips a nut in its claw and squawks to chill
A rival, which flees, so Raab squawked at the EU
And also at the Chancellor to rule and shoo.
     Rees-Mogg quotes *Proverbs* to confirm a split:
"As a dog returneth to his vomit,
So a fool returneth to his folly" –
Fools repeat their folly and aren't sorry.
So on the Ship of Fools, the fools accuse
The wise of repeating their 'foolish' views.
Fools think the wise foolish, don't recognise
200   That folly's best recognised by the wise.
     The Government is split again, all squeal.
Most polled think the UK'll get a bad deal.
Another crisis summit on Tory
'No deal' will seek to unite the party.
It's clear there is a price that must be paid
For the Brexiteers' fantasy to trade
Solo and control the UK's borders,
They look back to Britannia's – their ancestors' –
Rule of the waves and of a great Empire
210   That all humanity did once admire,
That spanned a quarter of the world with bands
And coloured red on maps its conquered lands.

There is no room for national sovereignty
In an interconnected world where an economy
Is built on international trade and on
Intergovernmental cooperation.
The EU's the best model for such leadership.
The UK's giving up its member's grip
On the world's biggest trading bloc for freight
220   To have other states' governments dictate
The terms of its trade and increase red tape:
Sixteen thousand civil servants to reshape.

    The Ship of State ploughs on, and all pretend
If there's 'no deal' all will be well in the end.
It is the way of fools to hope all's well
Though it's chaos and paradise is Hell.
The wise man looks at the kitchen table
And keeps reserves of food if he's able.
Some ask if there's a mandate to crash out.
230   The UK Government hoped to end doubt
About the terms of the UK's exit
From Europe by mid-October, but it
Seems this deadline might slip to give more time.
The EU insists that 'time up' will chime
At the end of October. All looks bad.

    Will May fall to her knees, passionately sad,
And make an impassioned plea to Juncker
In Norman French – crying in a *clameur*
For justice from the Duke of Normandy,
240   William the Conqueror, an ancient plea:
"Haro! à l'aide, mon Prince, on me fait tort" –
"Justice! Come to my aid, my prince, please, for
Someone does me wrong", the *Clameur de Haro*,
The Norman Cry for Justice; "Please bestow
Protection for our right to a good deal
As we helped chart the European feel
And build the hugely prosperous EU
As William would have wanted us to do."

Did May *clameur* to French Macron as well?
250   Did 'Haro' recall Harold and how he fell?
May's tried to keep the Union together,
And her Cabinet, in 'no-deal' weather.

A hurricane of words fills the air waves,
On radio, TV, phones, delirium raves.
Brexit's a historic mistake, some rage.
Endless arguments whirl, storm and rampage.
Indecision makes dire predictions burst.
Some have blind faith the EU will blink first
At the last minute, that's a delusion.
260   The EU knows May's plan is dead and gone.
The main rule of the EU's single
Market is: goods, services, people
And capital, the four freedoms, cannot
Be divided, but the Chequers plan's plot
Is to seek to divide the four, rebel.
The Chequers plan to stay in the single
Market for trade in goods (not services),
People and capital, like picked cherries,
Partially in the single market, a bit
270   Like the EEC, is now a target.
      Barnier'll offer a partnership (seems keen)
To the UK "such as there's never been"
With a third country. He has to appear
To the twenty-seven both fair and clear.
He means an off-the-shelf, not a bespoke,
Model the UK can choose to invoke:
The South Korea, Norway, Ukraine, Efta,
Mexico, Switzerland or Canada
Model. France says that the UK must pay
280   For access to the single market's sway.
      Now Barnier says the Chequers plan is flawed,
It would create bureaucracy and fraud
And separating goods from services

39

Would kill the European project, he says,
And end the single market. His strong frown
Threatens to bring the May Government down
Unless it now makes a new concession.
She says, "I won't make compromises on
Chequers that are not in the national
290   Interest." (So that means there can be several
Concessions *in* the national interest?)
      The Brexiteers oppose the Chequers test:
·   Too many concessions – Common Rule Book,
Subservience to the ECJ's outlook,
Customs union in all but name – that's steep.
Davis says that the Chequers plan will keep
The UK under the EU. His cartel
Is the South-Korean and Australian model.
      Remainers too oppose the Chequers plan.
300   If May gets it past the EU how can
She get it through Parliament? Your poet, then
Standing with Cleverly in a country garden,
Hears, "A deal looks fifty-fifty. If there's
No deal and Labour brings a motion that dares
To call to stay in the EU" – a frown –
"We could not muster the strength to vote it down."
So the UK may stay in the EU.
      Macron counters a 'no deal' by just two
Concentric circles: the EU would be
310   A point at the centre of a circle of free
EU member states and of a wider-splay
Circle of associates and the UK,
Like the outer circle in Dante's Hell.
Forty French scallop boats ram on a swell
UK boats towing dredge nets for scallops
Twelve miles off France where the UK have net drops
But not the French, who're banned from their own seas.
Raab says the UK'll keep part of 'the squeeze',
The thirty-nine-billion-pound exit fee,

320   If the Chequers plan's blocked and 'no deal' breaks free.
          May goes to sub-Saharan southerners
And reveals the UK's trading partners
Who'll replace EU states: South Africa
And, wait for it, Nigeria and Kenya.
The UK's two-way trade with the EU rounds
Five hundred and fifty-four billion pounds,
With Africa's just thirteen billion. Where's
The rest coming from when the UK glares
And walks away and has to make up loss?
330   Asked if the UK'll be more prosperous
After Brexit than if she'd refused to go,
May refuses to answer, must be 'no'.
          There are plots to chuck Chequers, then oust May.
Johnson and Rees-Mogg are eager for the fray.
No urgency on the talks, no way through;
All want to chuck Chequers, which the EU
Has already rejected and Parliament
Won't accept as it does not have the assent
Of Labour's criteria. So it's now said
340   That May's flogging a plan that's already dead
As Chequers won't happen. Some Tories call
For a new plan and a new PM, but all
Can see the Government can't deliver
A deal for Brexit that most will prefer.
May's plan's under siege at home and abroad.
It seems the EU'll put it to the sword.
The Chequers deal was a grand delusion,
Brexiteers sneer and Remainers blacken,
Want a Free-Trade Agreement that would steal
350   Canada or Norway, or a 'no deal'
That would take all back to WTO
Rules, and would lay the economy low.

The Ship of State is riven through and through
By the infighting of its murderous crew.

Can the captain steer between the turbulent
Rocks where the sea seethes in whirling ferment?
Where beyond these rocks is the route to paradise,
To a wondrous land of plenty, fire and ice?
Are the captain and crew too riven to cross the sea
360   And transport the Ship to a land of prosperity?

Canto VII
Mutiny

Sing, Muse, of how the antics, push-and-shove,
Of the Brexiteer Johnson who many love
And who some loathe with a ferocity,
Upset millions, destroyed his family,
And how 'chuck Chequers' threatened May's pedestal.
    The EU's senior Irish official
Has told Grayling that if there is 'no deal' no
Other agreements will protect the slow
UK economy. Ignoring this "view"
Grayling's sent twenty-seven letters to EU
Member-states asking for side deals – if there's
'No deal' on aviation and haulage, scares.
Now Barnier confronts Raab with severe zeal,
"There'll be no side deals if there is 'no deal'.
If there is 'no deal', there's no trust." Raab tells
Barnier the EU must order – he swells –
The Irish Government to reinstate
The Northern Irish border for all freight
If there's 'no deal'. Barnier's in a furious strop,
No progress is made on the Irish backstop.
The EU should not border and confine,
Or man customs checks that would undermine
The Good-Friday Agreement and restore
Irish nationalism and the gun law
Of the murderous IRA. He's provoked,
The EU negotiator's been poked.
    Johnson's working on a leadership bid.
The court jester and fool in a florid
Article in *The Telegraph* is pained:
The Raab-Barnier fight's fixed, as preordained
As a bout between Big Daddy and Giant Haystacks:
The UK canvased, thrown after attacks,
With twelve stars circling round its swooning head,

10

20

30

Comatose, pulverised and filled with dread.
Thirty-nine billion pounds has to be paid
For two-thirds of diddly-squat – no trade,
Nothing; and tying the UK's routine
To the EU's standards on goods will mean
Going into battle with a white flag.
40   By agreeing to a common rule book's gag
The UK can't compete and must forswear
The project of global Britain. Beware,
The EU's manipulated the Irish
Border and several pro-EU British
Ministers to keep the UK in the net
Of the customs union and single market.
Arguably there *is* a border today,
Two jurisdictions, each with a different sway.
We have the Common Travel Area
50   But the Chequers plan is a disaster.
Some want to stop true Brexit. The UK
Needs a Free-Trade deal – not a new Norway
Or EEA – which would scrap the Irish
Backstop. Johnson says the EU's no wish
To fix the Irish border, but what did
He do to solve the problem when he hid
In the Foreign Office for two years? What
Border challenge did he make? Diddly-squat.
As a peacock fans its tail and displays
60   And struts around with a hundred eyes ablaze,
So Johnson preened dazzling phrases in print
And paraded his tousled hair and squint.
Did he say Irish peace could be capsized?
    A major figure in Leave, he advised
The public to leave though Ireland looks bleak.
A hack journalist on five grand a week,
He's no leader. What a waste of two years.
He's manoeuvring to force May out in tears
And walk into 10 Downing Street, but frown:

70 He who wields the knife never wears the crown.
   May says the jester's article offers
 No new ideas, the UK needs (she purrs)
 Serious leadership with a serious plan,
 Not a clown, a buffoon, a charlatan.
 But the Chequers deal's more unpopular
 Than the Poll Tax. The rebels, with *hauteur*,
 Have pledged to wreck the Chequers plan, dissent.
 It won't be accepted in Parliament.

 Now it's announced Johnson will be divorced.
80 He lived apart from his wife before he was forced
 To vacate the grace-and-favour mansion
 In Carlton Gardens, his sickened wife's gone
 Because of his fourth affair with a Tory
 Aide, a blonde. He's dined her in Rules' cosy
 Corner on Valentine's Day, two police
 Sitting peeved by the door, keeping the peace,
 A Merrie Englander, Lord of Misrule
 Who's made two mistresses pregnant; a fool.
 His Turkish ancestry's coloured his view
90 Of marriage: Muslims can have four wives, he too
 Feels it's unreasonable for a man to be
 Confined to one woman and not be more free.
 He's "getting his skeletons out of the closet",
 "Clearing the decks" – that's wrong, he wouldn't get
 To break up his marriage just so he can challenge
 May for the leadership (and take revenge
 For missing out last time amid ill will)
 Without a scandal. Will the divorce kill
 Off voters' affection for his 'open book'?
100 Will the public still love his scruffy look
 And uncombed hair when he's a serial
 Two-timer as well as a humorous 'pal'?
 May's at risk. He's split party and country,
 Now he's split his long-standing family.

He's made promises and can't deliver,
He's a selfish, irresponsible wrecker.
To some his divorce confirms what many drool:
That this witty court jester's just a fool.
Johnson's shown on a giant screen asleep
110   At the Oval Test and's booed: a loathsome heap.

Now in *The Telegraph* Johnson compares May
To a suicide bomber who's wrapped the UK
In a suicide vest and handed the detonator
To Barnier, to blow up and spread terror.
But it's *he*, not May, who's destroyed the country
With his call to leave the EU. The Tory
Party's in open civil war. Some screech
His metaphor's "disgusting", others preach
That he's now the heir apparent, the King
120   Over the Water. But he's becoming
A sideshow: colourful hyperbole,
Unmeasured language but no plan to re-
Place the Chequers proposal with new law.
    The Eurosceptics' Report's laid before
A meeting of fifty rebels, enough
To trigger a leadership challenge and bluff
May. A gasp when what it includes is revealed:
A grandiose Star-Wars missile-defence shield;
An expeditionary force to defend
130   The Falklands; and tariffs-on-foods to end,
Which will destroy British agriculture's brands.
Johnson, Rees-Mogg and Bone sit heads in hands
And can't believe they're reading what's been dished.
All say the Report should not be published
Because of its undeliverable prate.
The Brexiteers have left it all too late.
Just as jackdaws and magpies wait for bread
And look and turn away as it's rejected,
So the extremist Brexiteers declined

140   To swallow the print fed to each one's mind.
Now they don't have the numbers to get their way.
    Now the negotiation has full sway.
Now Johnson rows back on his outspoken rave.
Thinking he may be digging his own grave,
He says he wants to challenge May's Brexit
Policy, rather than oust her. He's split,
He's overreached and ruined his country
With mistakes he's now seeking to bury.
Receiving an award in America,
150   He says, "My strategy is to litter
My career with so many decoy mistakes
No one knows which one to attack." Each shakes
With laughter as he plays the fool, mawkish,
Pretending his folly is not foolish.
    What is ahead in our uncertain time?
Chaotic 'no deal', lorry backlogs, crime
And aircraft groundings? A co-operative
'No deal' deal whose WTO rules give
A security treaty? Transition,
160   Canada-plus and a border that's on
The Irish Sea but no tariffs? Norway,
Which would mean staying in the EEA?
Transition and Chequers, May's plan to align
Through a common rule book and be benign?
A 'blind Brexit', details after leaving?
Or staying in the EU, remaining?
Eight possible outcomes bemuse, some feel:
Does it boil down to Chequers or 'no deal'?
Confusion reigns in a febrile atmosphere.
170   Some look in crystal balls and are then clear:
A withdrawal deal can soon be agreed
With the rights of all citizens guaranteed,
An Irish-border backstop with some clout,
Thirty-nine billion pounds trickling out
And a commitment to negotiate

A trade deal by the transition's end date.
If May's deal's voted down, the Queen will ask
Corbyn to form a government, a task
That may result in a third general
180   Election in three years and a constitutional
Crisis to find someone who could lead the UK
Past the end-of-March Brexit Deadline-Day.
What a nightmare the brash Brexiteers await.
Zeus, please save the EU from such a fate.

An oaf is shouting on the Ship of State
Incoherent orders to the master's mate
Who's still listening to the captain, his boss.
The crew are bailing as waves dip and toss
And swamp the deck with water that runs down
190   Into the hold, passengers wail, "We'll drown."
But still the ship ploughs on through steepling waves,
Its deck crowded with fools as the wind raves.
They cling to railings and long for the land
Of plenty that awaits them, on whose sand
They'll disembark near a fertile river's source
When the captain, oaf and crew agree their course.

Canto VIII
Salzburg Summit

Sing, Muse, of Salzburg and of the EU's
Summit for twenty-seven member-states whose
Leaders May's a long time hoped to address
And of a UK-EU deal's progress.
Sing, Muse, of the Chequers plan's rejection,
Sing of self-blindness and self-delusion,
Of miscalculation and foolishness.
    Barnier still wants a border to transgress
The Irish Sea, breaking the United
10   Kingdom in two. He has now rejected
May's plan that the whole UK should stay on
In the single market and customs union
For goods but not services as cherry-
Picking – some Brussels cakes have cherries. He
Has proposed a third plan: goods would be tracked
On bar-codes on shipping containers packed
Under 'trusted-trade' schemes administered
By registered companies that partnered,
And would not endanger, the single market
20   So May could survive long enough to get
A deal with Brussels to avoid 'no deal'.
    Now eighty MPs meet, one says with zeal,
"If no 'Chuck Chequers', then chuck May." But, sir,
Changing the pilot won't change the weather.
They'll block a deal based on the Chequers plan
And split the Tory party, chuck and ban.
'Chuck Chequers'? No. There is no plan or view
But Chequers being discussed by the EU.
    Barnier says a Brexit deal can be done
30   In two months, by mid-November. He's spun,
Barnier's changed his tone but not his content,
He's keeping May in power, it's evident
He doesn't want Johnson, who'd plunge the EU

Into chaos; but won't change the rules or his view.
The negotiation's on EU terms.
Jaguar Land Rover, one of many firms,
Sees tens of thousands of their jobs at risk
If there's 'no deal', whose impact will be brisk.
A 'no-deal' Brexit could be as disastrous
40   As the financial crash, that was parlous.
House prices could crash by a third, the Bank-
Of-England Governor says from a think-tank.
A soft Brexit will bring the best of times
To the UK, 'no deal' the worst of climes.
The UK's economy will suffer
If there's 'no deal', the IMF aver.

      Brexit's become a cautionary tale
On how Euroscepticism will fail
That could help save the EU from a wave
50   Of Eurosceptic populism (its grave)
When the EU is expanding non-stop
Into a United States of Europe:
Juncker has planned an armed ten-thousand-strong
Border force with power to detain a throng
Of migrants and deport failed asylum
Seekers. A Europe, muscular, not glum,
Will be a global player and impose
Its view on an unstable world and foes
With military might. Its states will hand
60   More powers to Brussels to unite the land,
To integrate and stop their vetoings
On EU foreign policy rulings
So the EU has a grandiose world-view.

      Poor May does not know how she will get through
The crucial Salzburg summit that now looms.
Will mighty Europe speak with one voice that booms?
Now Raab rings Barnier and reports they are
Closing in on a deal – now near, once far –
And can bring the talks to a successful

70   Conclusion after the magical pull
           Of the snow-capped Alps' blue-skied and sunlit
           Cold bracing air at the Salzburg summit.

           In Salzburg after four hours and a crunch –
           Heated talk of migration, then a lunch
           When a fractious Macron tore up Tusk's plan
           For a November Brexit summit, a ban
           To make the Brexit process move faster –
           In the room in the *Felsenreitschule*
           Where in *The Sound of Music* children sigh
80   "So long, farewell, *auf Wiedersehen*, goodbye"
           May speaks to the twenty-seven leaders
           At a large oval table, and dinner's
           Wiener Schnitzel and old Austrian wine,
           And says unless a deal is reached in line
           With the Chequers plan in November, then on cue
           The UK'll walk away from the EU
           With 'no deal' and no extending of talks
           Or second referendum despite the squawks.
               She seems to be using the same words as in
90   An article she wrote in the Berlin
           Daily *Die Welt*, not persuading, and she's
           Rejected Barnier's revised offer – a "wheeze" –
           On Ireland to use bar-codes, without seeing
           The text, two mistakes like her threatening
           To walk away, and she's irritated
           The twenty-seven, ignored what they had said,
           Their call for amendments, she's come across
           As inflexible, she's talked like a boss,
           She's said of Chequers, "Take it or leave it."
100   She's clung to the illusion that they'd split
           Or cave in, and they've bristled in their skin.
           She's been given ten minutes, they've listened in
           Silence and can't debate till the next day.
           She's said it's her deal or 'no deal', the way

Of siding with her Eurosceptic flank
To neuter it and dodge walking the plank.
Just as a white dove perches by its cote
And observes a sparrowhawk preparing to float
And swoop, and anxiously edges inside,
110   So May edged out of the room before she died.
      Has she put her survival and party
Before national well-being? An icy
Tusk and the Belgian and Dutch leaders each
Seek to ease the mandate on Barnier to reach
A deal, but Juncker, the German and French
Leaders still stick to EU rules, and wrench.
Juncker says that a deal is still far off.
Barnier's line is still an eloquent scoff.
      Next afternoon the twenty-seven EU
120   Leaders meet without the UK and construe
They cannot back May's plan as it won't work,
The economic partnership would irk
And undermine the EU. The Irish
Backstop is still a problem, and their wish.
Merkel and Macron both rebuff the plan
As unacceptable. Macron, no fan
Of May's, says that UK voters were duped
Into voting Leave by liars, corralled and cooped.
Fox had said reaching a free-trade deal that's blessed
130   By the EU would be "one of the easiest
Deals in human history". Completely wrong.
Tusk says the UK's plan will not last long
Unless it makes more concessions, that's key.
If not, the October summit will see
Talks fail and a further November summit
Abandoned, along with deals for Brexit.
      Rejected, May looks shocked, shaken, nervous
And at a press conference furious.
She says her plan's the only credible
140   Proposition on the summit table.

She's moved her red lines as the Council said
But the twenty-seven ambushed her instead.
The UK's misunderstood the EU.
Her plan ended in failure, no breakthrough
As she cherry-picked, only a breakdown.
Tusk posts on Instagram a mocking frown:
He offers May a cake stand, the caption is,
"Piece of cake perhaps? Sorry, no cherries."
He's disrespected her, it's a nightmare.

150   It's all gone wrong for May, it's hard to bear
Such a harsh reaction, and to believe
Cherry-picking is allowed was naïve,
Delusional, a fantasy, just wrong.
She and her adviser Robbins have long
Been living within a fools' paradise
Of 'good-for-me', not 'what-they'll-do' advice.

     The next day she fights back in a broadcast
From 10 Downing Street demanding a fast
Explanation, as the EU has to give

160   In an Article-50 narrative.
She seems in denial, she's learned nothing.
She blusters, speaks angrily, threatening.
She demands respect's shown to the UK,
Says EU residents there can all stay,
Then freezes all talks until the EU
Comes up with a proposal that'll outdo
The Chequers plan. She threatens a 'no deal'
If the twenty-seven don't give ground and kneel.
The UK press approves, defeat now turns

170   Into glorious victory – Boudicca sacks and burns,
Dunkirk's turned into mighty British power,
The Battle of Britain, May's finest hour.

     Tusk says May's Salzburg statement – her curfew –
Was tough and uncompromising. The EU
Supports Barnier's strong view of the single
Market and Ireland; a deal's still possible

If May makes new concessions. What did she expect?
It was obvious the EU would reject.
There is surprise she was surprised and fumes.
180   She's said there is an *impasse*. 'No deal' looms.

There's been a diplomatic disaster,
On the scale of the Suez crisis, after
The Salzburg summit and MPs attack,
There's pressure to dump the Chequers plan and back
A looser free-trade deal with the EU.
But this may break up – dump – the UK too.
  · Northern Ireland and Scotland may fall away
From a restless and fragmenting UK.
      Now Starmer, unscripted, says Labour will
190   Support a second referendum. A thrill
Surges through the Labour conference hall,
And a standing ovation speaks for all.
(Elsewhere May says she'll cut UK taxes
To the lowest in the G20 countries.)
Now on the platform Corbyn speaks his dream:
A utopia round a wonderful stream
Of gushing liquid money funding hordes:
The end of student debt; workers on boards;
Shares given away; the nationalising
200   Of water, energy, railways and a ring
Of thirty-seven promises startling
In their grandiose sweep, sadly costing
A trillion pounds and afforded from the glow
Of a crock of gold at the foot of a rainbow.
      And now for utopia's reality:
Shops to let, factories closed, derelict firms empty;
Inflation up, pension funds hit, the poor
Begging for help, Labour's give-away more
A fantasy of plenty without price,
210   A mass cheering in a fools' paradise.
      Johnson's now called the Chequers plan "deranged".

He's "irrelevant", "offensive", unchanged.
And Corbyn says he'll sink any deal May
Strikes with the EU, so there'll be delay.
A second referendum is ahead
As voters were told untruths that were spread
By word of mouth as they entered the booths,
As oil on troubled waters calms and soothes:
Three hundred and fifty million a week
220   For the NHS, frictionless trade to peak
With the EU and Ireland, and trade deals
The day after the UK leaves and seals.
Now Johnson wants to rip up the backstop
Agreement with the EU, and to lop
Its binding force, and trust in the UK.
Would the EU allow him to betray
What the UK signed on the eighth of December
And replace it with Super Canada
That would split the UK with the backstop
230   If honouring the law's not for the chop?
(Saying the UK can cancel its laws
And treaties it's signed up to, for a cause,
And obligations that it doesn't like,
Is a lie that amounts to going on strike.)
     Voters are more discerning now, and see
A second referendum's necessary.
And your poet sees why, looking ahead
Via a video with a one-world thread,
Bilderberg and the Digital New World
240   *Order*, as a borderless planet's unfurled:
Forty-four minutes on e-Estonia,
Where the Soviets' left a digital area,
Where all have an ID card whose chip hoards
Their banking, medical and tax records,
Their passport, driving-licence, SOS.
And behold the future, a borderless
Digitally-connected, interdependent,

World-wide society with sensors present
On all house doors, vast metal armies, lots
250   Of artificial-intelligence robots
Who, as in Saudi-Arabia's NEOM town
Which has cost half a trillion dollars down
To build, are digitally-controlled to work,
To mow, shop and 'man' computers, and lurk
Between jobs till they are needed, to wait,
So all are working within a World State;
Estonia's pioneered this AI 'mind'
But France is next, it's just five years behind.
      Your poet's glimpsed the future and knew then
260   That Brexit can't be allowed to happen,
Nor Trump's rejection of global order,
Which is at odds with the borderless venture.
The doctrine of patriotism's dead,
No heretics will be tolerated
In this digital World State in which all
Use ID cards through each spring and each fall,
Lead global lives in a borderless state
In a universal democracy that's run late.

The Ship of State is running out of food.
270   The fools cry out for stalks that can be chewed
But the crew are too busy arguing
To attend to the needs of the starving.
The fools' water bottles are now empty.
They thirst and want land to appear quickly,
To loom out of the horizon's heat haze
So they can escape from the fierce sun's blaze
And sip clear water at the bubbling spring
That will be on the shore when the crew bring
The Ship into the shallows to scrape on stones,
280   And judder to a halt, jolting their bones,
And they'll jump out and wade, and lie down in
Vegetation, amid fruit-trees and grin –

O, how much longer till, like a *mirage*,
A paradisal lake shimmers from *bocage*?

Canto IX
Party Conference

Sing, Muse, of the party-conference glee,
Of Johnson's collision with May as he
Sets out his stall as next PM, to shine;
Sing how May jigged her party into line
And how stern Barnier would not compromise,
For how could sunset be merged with sunrise?
Sing how events slid towards a 'no deal'.
  Witness a convention meeting get real:
May's booed and heckled by her own party
When explaining her Chequers plan simply
And walks off with no standing ovation.
Cabinet ministers are phoned by Johnson,
Who says, if PM, he'd delay Brexit
Six months to reset talks about the split
So the UK can gain the upper hand –
But why would the EU agree that stand?
  No mention of the delay when he speaks
At a fringe meeting to supporting cliques
And calls for more housing and low tax when
The NHS now needs twenty billion.
He says: chuck Chequers, scrap backstop, make free-
Trade deals for Chequers is just a "fantasy",
An outrage and May should be arrested
Under the fourteenth-century Statute of (long dead)
Praemunire, which bans all foreign courts
Or governments from having (he snorts)
Jurisdiction in England. He is sketchy,
This Statute was repealed in nineteen-sixty-
Seven. There's no detail, just empty headlines.
He speaks as a Messiah, he combines
Making an alternative PM's speech
With appealing to the party members' reach.
He makes a pitch without a rival plan,

And seeks to come across as 'I'm the Man'.
His talk will be forgotten in two days.
    But now the Cabinet demands that May's
PMship should be limited, that she
Should set a date to quit. She won't agree.
May's to speak at the conference. Some scoff:

40   Last year she had an unstoppable cough,
Stuck letters fell off the wall behind her,
She was served a P45 by a joker.
She needs a vision of where she sees (not fears)
The UK will be in five or ten years.
    May puppet-jigs in for her conference speech,
To Abba's 'Dancing Queen', all set to preach,
And calls a halt to eight years' spending cuts,
The years of austerity and 'bank shuts'
(For which twenty billion pounds must be found

50   From tax hikes to pay off the austere mound
Of debt that will crush the just-managing
So it will seem austerity's returning).
She signals that better days will beckon
Prosperity to post-Brexit Britain,
And "backs" business with sensible *finesse*
Following Johnson's foul-mouthed "F— business".
Just as a swan glides elegantly to bank,
Climbs out and ungainly spreads its wings to clank
And then waddles, so May pranced in her dance

60   And beamed at the audience with a nervous glance.
    She sells her plan without saying 'Chequers':
The UK'll strike new trade deals as partners,
Renew its role in the world and control
Its money, laws and borders and keep whole
The United Kingdom. (But that's a falsehood:
Goods, agriculture, food and fisheries would
Be governed by a common rule book's creep
Overseen by the ECJ, and keep
The UK locked inside the EU so

70   It could not strike new free-trade deals and grow.)
She says the UK has strengths: English thrives
As the global language, the UK drives
The Commonwealth and has a permanent seat
With the UN Security Council's *élite*;
Three of the world's top ten universities;
And the winners of more Nobel prizes
Than any other country save the US,
And it's invented the internet: progress.
She could have said its scientists unlocked
80   Gravity and evolution, unblocked
Penicillin, decoded DNA
And pioneered democracy – the way
Of *Magna Carta*, where the English found
That genius thrives in freedom when it's crowned;
And that as the world's financial hub, quite free,
It has the world's fifth biggest economy
And the third largest development budget, though
It's the second biggest military in NATO.
She doesn't say the economy'll take a hit
90   Or that there's no dividend for Brexit;
Or that 'Better Off Alone' is a fantasy.
She leaves to the strumming of 'Mr Blue Sky'.

Now May's ringing EU leaders to close
A deal by the coming summit, and propose
The UK stays in a customs union
With the EU for a limited duration
And follows EU tariffs to prevent
The Irish-Sea border the EU scent.
     Tusk, President of the European Council,
100   Counters with the EU's own proposal,
An unprecedented trade, security
And foreign policy pact that would be
Similar to its Canada agreement,
A Canada plus-plus-plus deal, more recent,

To be a no-tariff free-trade deal on
All goods with add-on co-operation
In security and foreign policy;
The full details would be thrashed out stress-free
During the twenty-one-month transition.
110   10 Downing Street's swift in its rejection.
It would mean the annexing of Northern Ireland
By the EU. Eurosceptics grandstand.
(They regard the Irish border as just
A political issue Barnier's thrust.
So long as Great Britain is tariff-free
Northern Ireland should cope separately.)
Somehow May danced her party together
And Johnson's star looks to have set further.
(On social media he miswrites 'backstop'
120   As a seriously-confused 'backdrop'.)
Robbins is having more talks in Brussels
And May has again to head off a shambles,
Reject an EU offer that Northern
Ireland should stay in the customs union
Or have a border down the Irish Sea
Which would divide the UK permanently.
     How did a law exercise such duress?
How did the UK get into such a mess?
How did May come to accept that Northern
130   Ireland should stay tied – if no solution
To a hard border can be found – to EU
Rules? She thought she was offering a few
Meaningless assurances on Northern
Ireland which turned into a ratification
That's legally binding with treaty force,
A guarantee from an official source,
An irrevocable undertaking
That seems to have been a misunderstanding.
The December Joint Progress Report's spin
140   In paragraph forty-nine states that in

The absence of full agreement the UK
"Will maintain full alignment" (in its own way)
With single market and customs union rules.
    The DUP protested, and the fools
Contradicted this in paragraph fifty,
Which promised "no new regulatory
Barriers" between and "unfettered access"
By Northern Ireland to the UK's largesse
And to the Republic of Ireland's 'align'.
150   A first version of paragraph forty-nine
Stated Northern Ireland alone would stay
In full alignment with EU rules' say.
The DUP replaced it as it went to press.
    The EU's returned to this version's dress.
The EU hardened all this up in March:
Northern Ireland must remain under the arch
Of the customs union and single market
In breach of the Good-Friday Agreement, yet
Also of the unity of the UK,
160   Which would break up to general dismay.
O how unforgiving are our treaty wits,
One misunderstanding and a country splits.
    May says there'll be no Brussels deal unless
The EU gives ground and makes good progress
To a precise future framework for trade.
But her adviser Robbins is dismayed
In Brussels after talks ended early:
He sits drinking red wine at five-thirty,
Alone in a Brussels pub as Barnier
170   Blandly offers that Great Britain should stay
In the customs union and Northern Ireland
In the single market with a border manned
Down the Irish Sea till a trade deal wriggles free
(If it ever does) or until technology
Can advance and return the border to where
It is today (if it ever can) in thin air.

That's the offer, will that be the final deal?
180   May needs to watch her back as the Irish squeal.
The DUP'd turn backstop to backstab,
Their leader Foster will block any grab.
She seems to want a bribe for her support,
Another billion from May and she'll be bought.
It's the whole people that count, not her patch;
The welfare of the nation, not her snatch.
She seems to put ambition before country.
Lord, what fools these strange politicians be.
      May chairs the Inner Cabinet meeting
190   On Thursday and says Barnier's demanding
The UK should stay – until a trade deal's done
In a customs union till 2021 –
Shackled in a transition agreement
That's extended a year, a new event
That will add fifteen billion pounds to the bill,
Which has made all the Brexiteers feel ill
As they fear the UK will now be trapped,
That free-trade deals and control will be scrapped
In a never-ending limbo Brexit,
200   An endless backstop that has no limit.
      That is her stance, will that be the final deal?
The furious Brexiteers seek to repeal.
May now says the extension must be time-
Limited, sensing they feel it's a crime.

The shape of the final deal now leaks out
From Cabinet to the MPs, who doubt.
Your poet sips champagne with Priti Patel,
Who says ferociously in a hotel,
"We're not getting the Brexit we want, Great Britain
210   Will stay – remain – in the customs union.
May's lied to us. She asked Davis to work
On Canada plus and also that jerk
Robbins to prepare the Chequers plan, to ghost.

She's disgusting. And two-fisted. She's toast.
It's shameful." What does she mean by Brexit?
I smile at her Humpty-Dumpty exit:
When she uses a word it means exactly
What *she* chooses it to mean, like Humpty.

    May's got twenty-seven EU states' assent
220   And three-quarters of the UK's agreement
And just needs England, but if she cosies
Up to the EU she'll lose the English Tories,
And up to England she'll lose the EU.
It's impossible to see May's way through.
It's like Hunt boxed-in by the Chevening maze
With the EU's foreign ministers, and no ways
Out, heads in bewildering hedges, waving.
On all sides there are factions, all warring.
She's lost in a maze whose every path is blocked,
230   A prisoner in her own backstop choice, locked
In and feeling trapped, starting to panic,
Surrounded by chaos, hedged-in and sick.

    Sunday, the day the deal should have been agreed.
Raab's rushed to Brussels to block a legal deed.
Robbins was about to sign up the UK
To a customs union in March with no end day
And enshrine into law now, to be included
In the final deal, a backstop that would embed
Northern Ireland without end in the EU,
240   A backstop now to a March backstop: two.
Raab meets Barnier and unagrees the deed
That Robbins, exceeding his brief, had agreed,
Says a customs deal must have an end date
And a break clause so the UK can abrogate.
Barnier won't budge, the backstop's law. Dismay,
Raab knows 'no deal' means the backstop goes away
And Northern Ireland has a hard border.
Robbins agreed to lock the UK further,
Into joint defence and security ties

250   Under EU control, which would compromise
        The UK's intelligence-gathering power.
           The talks collapse after just over an hour
        And the meeting of civil-servant 'Sherpas'
        Who prepare documents for summits' handlers
        Has been cancelled so there will now be no
        Text to discuss on Wednesday; a big blow.
        England's on the verge of its worst defeat
        Since the Saxons at Hastings, who the Normans beat.
           In Parliament May makes a statement *before*
260   The summit, on the state of the Brexit war.
        There's division, each group wants her to drop
        Her support for a 'no-end-date' backstop
        And sees no way through and 'no deal' looming.
        A third of the Cabinet meets for plotting,
        To end the Chequers plan over spicy
        Pizza Leadsom's organised secretly.
        The new Attorney-General Cox says any
        Withdrawal deal would become a treaty
        And be impossible to unpick or deflate.
270   All agree any backstop must have an end date.
        The wording 'temporary' would have no
        Binding in law, and the Chief Whip calls whoa,
        Says a customs deal without an-end consent
        Would not be voted for in Parliament.
           It seems that Brexit's undeliverable.
        The negotiators can't square the circle,
        The leaders at the Brussels summit won't say
        That if there's 'no deal' the backstop 'goes away'.
        There's a border along Northern Ireland,
280   And an isolated UK will withdraw as planned
        Behind the walls of a fortified boundary
        And must still pay a whopping exit fee.
        It's make-or-break week for May, but all's not well
        With the Brexiteers' plan as they can't sell
        It to the Northern-Irish and stop their pain.

It's widely said the people should think again.
Major says that political princelings – he
Means both Johnson and Gove – will never be
Forgiven for their false promises if
290   Brexit goes wrong, and that the Brexit vote – sniff –
Was a colossal misjudgement. There are more
Calls for a second referendum, for
The SNP will support such a course.
    During the Coalition, with some force
Osborne, Clegg and Alexander advised
Cameron not to hold the criticised
Referendum, but he waved them aside,
Believing the election would provide
Another coalition and that stubborn
300   Liberals would not let a referendum happen –
And the Conservative victory meant he
Would have to keep his promise to oversee
A referendum he could not suppress.
He had been stuck with his own cleverness.
What a fool for being in that position
And misjudging the outcome of the election.
    Now the leaders of Brexit have fled the scene:
Cameron, who led the UK to a mean
Calamity, midway between extremes,
310   Hides in his shepherd's hut and his day-dreams,
Writes self-justifying memoirs for – hey –
Eight hundred thousand pounds, but does not say
His political battles were genteel
When set beside his decision to appeal
To the worst of the Tory party's shades
And launch a crisis that will last decades,
And now, having gambled at silencing
His back-bench critics and walked out leaving
Chaos behind him, he's bored and would seek
320   To swan back into government and speak
As Foreign Secretary with an intent

That smacks of arrogant entitlement;
    Farage, whose poster showed an endless queue
Of Syrians entering the UK – untrue –
Is a radio host who now cuts callers off
As soon as they approach the truth and scoff;
Rees-Mogg, who looks like a ghost in Dickens'
Christmas Carol and haunts radio stations
With plausible half-truths in a mournful drawl;
330   Johnson, who has now abdicated all
Responsibility to hack – and laugh –
Out articles for *The Daily Telegraph*;
And Davis, who met Barnier without papers
And for just six hours in six months – jeepers –
And whose ill-considered concessions bound
The UK into its mess, mooches around
And says if he's PM he'll ban and chase
All EU planes from the UK's airspace –
Back to World War Two, and Biggles as well.
340   They've left us trapped in a circle of Hell
As they sail to their distant paradise.
    O how blind is the politicians' advice.
They've misled the people into a vile bog,
How worthy of ostracism is their fog.
How convinced of their rectitude they've been,
And how arrogantly they pose and preen.
And how their decisions look a misfit
As May arrives at a new EU summit.

The Ship of State now rolls from side to side.
350   There's no trace of coast where the captain-guide
Pointed at the horizon's haze and yelled,
"Land ahoy, mariners." He's now been felled,
Has a new mutiny begun, or did
A wave crash on the deck where he's just slid?
Clinging to rails all scan the distant mist
For the ship's destination, not seeing its list.

There can't be crocodiles and cholera,
Or poisonous snakes, in that utopia.
The Ship of State is dipping and swaying,
360   The fools are crying out their deep yearning
For the paradise their leaders promised,
That's hidden in mist and may not exist.

Canto X
Brussels' Rejection

Sing, Muse, of October's Brussels summit,
Of wrestling with backstop, of the EU's twilit
Rejection of the Chequers plan that May
Persisted with, and conflict in Brussels that day.
And sing of the Cabinet's response to the draft
Withdrawal text and May's lack of statecraft.
Sing of anger, of hatred and shambles
And the sound of deep silence in Brussels.
    The day of decision and destiny
10   Dawns darkly, the day the deal was supposed to be
Signed when the Lisbon Treaty's Article 50 –
That seems to have been invoked too hastily –
Was triggered and with a swagger delivered.
May has to negotiate with the partnered
EU leaders and her own Cabinet.
It's time to face reality, admit
The EU's not a tyranny imposed
On Europe like Charlemagne's ill-disposed,
Or the Habsburgs' composite, Empires' laws
20   But a sacred principle, after wars,
Of European integration and peace,
And open borders so all threats can cease.
    May speaks to the leaders of the EU
Before dinner, but she says nothing new.
She calls for the backstop to be replaced
By a future relationship that's soundly based.
She couldn't get a UK-wide customs union
Through her Cabinet, so makes no mention.
She's irritated the EU leaders
30   By shifting the onus onto their shoulders –
Courage, trust and leadership are her calls.
Her plea for them to break the deadlock falls
On deaf ears, many are frustrated at

Lack of new ideas, slow progress, unclear chat.
　　Merkel says she didn't really understand
What May was saying or what she has planned.
She'll ask Barnier to explain everything.
May's lack of clarity is perplexing.
She wants to leave, it's not for the EU
40　　To set her up in solitary splendour, anew.
There'll be no November summit, no big day
To sign off a deal, but they give Barnier
A mandate to work on so May can tease
Out a new plan to be passed by MPs.
And a new EU summit will be due
As soon as Barnier says there's a breakthrough.
　　Now Tusk reads a draft statement affirming
Full confidence in Barnier, and all sitting
Twenty-seven EU leaders rap knuckles
50　　On the table to support Barnier's struggles.
　　Merkel's said the UK should be able to stay
In the single market another year, and pay
Into the EU one more year. Juncker's said
That the transition may be extended.
The extension was Robbins' idea, and May
Thrashed it out in Brexit Cabinet last Thursday –
There's been a May-Robbins *duumvirate*
Since Chequers – and asked Merkel to float it.
(The UK is supposed to take control
60　　But the EU's in control of this goal.)
May'd extend for three months as a year would cost
Fifteen billion pounds, that's more money lost;
But the extension would not be needed
If a deal on the future relationship's completed
By December 2020 – nor the backstop.
Complete the deal in time and the extras drop.
　　Integrationist Macron is the most
Awkward EU leader, he says (as a boast)
The EU's dealt with backstop technically –

70   It *won't* be time-limited – and must be
Just a political issue for May
To deal with in Cabinet in the UK.
There should not be concessions by the EU
Because the UK has an unsolved issue.
As a cockerel struts round its coop and crows
And all the hens, alert, strike a still pose,
So Macron is in charge and all defer
And many who listen nod and concur.
He is preparing for 'no deal'. The French
80   Senate's reinstated customs checks – a wrench –
On trade, livestock, product safety and powers
To control roads round ports and queues for hours
Both in France and in the Channel Tunnel.
Five EU leaders, including Merkel
And Macron, leave dinner, which has lasted
Just over an hour, and go out (well-fed)
For beers within Brussels' Grand-Place, without
Inviting May, who sits alone to pout,
Bitter in the echoing residence
90   Of the Ambassador to the EU, make sense
And lament her isolation while an old
Clock ticks towards exit. She's in the cold.
      That night Merkel and Macron urge Barnier
To give May legal guarantees that say
A deal would never impose or decree
A customs border down the Irish Sea,
Fearing May will not be able to sell
Such a border to her Cabinet as well
As her back-benchers and the DUP.
100   Barnier must show more creativity
And be more flexible in talks with May
To find a way for the whole of the UK
To enter a temporary customs union
With the EU, though progress is stubborn.
      The former Finnish PM Stubb, who hopes

To be President of the Commission, copes:
"The EU negotiation's been typical:
Phase one crisis; phase two chaos; phase three'll
Be a sub-optimal solution, a surprise
110   That can be sold to all as a compromise
With both sides claiming victory." But how
Will Brexit fare or will extra time allow
A second referendum to fanfare
So the UK can wake from this nightmare
Of an undeliverable Brexit and remain?
If a deal is reached there can't be a 'restrain'
Amendment in Parliament, and that alarms
Enraged Remainers, who are also up in arms.
       Juncker says 'no deal' would hurt the UK
120   And the EU, but it's not yet doomsday.
The process will go on, more prevarication
And more delay and exasperation
Among Brexiteers, and dismay. As six
Hundred and seventy thousand intermix
And march through London and call for the deal to be stopped
Raab says that the backstop must now be dropped
Or else the UK'll leave the EU on time.
May seems to be bogged down in endless slime.

Now all are shocked at the summit's outcome.
130   Forty-six MPs have sent letters that thrum
And demand a contest, two more are needed
For a vote of 'no confidence' in how May's led.
She's told to address the 1922
Committee – perhaps a 'show trial' and *coup*.
There's talk of May being in the "killing zone",
Of an "assassination", a "funeral" – her own.
      In a statement to Parliament she seems set –
"We're ninety-five per cent there" (as at *Market
Garden*, according to Montgomery) –
140   And faces down her critics confidently

With four steps: to give the UK-EU
Customs union legally-binding glue
To avoid a 'Northern Ireland only' backstop;
To extend the transition-period prop
But not indefinitely; UK access
For Northern Ireland's businesses to progress;
And Northern Ireland to stay tied to EU rules
If solving a hard border still befools.
Backstop is still an issue and has hardened,
150   Yet she says the EU's not to be threatened
With 'no deal'. It's clear she has no vision
And sees Brexit in terms of immigration,
A too-narrow interpretation that
Reflects her limits as a bureaucrat.
And there are nearly a thousand statutory
Instruments to be amended quickly
And laid before MPs before Brexit's end,
And less than six months in which to amend.
      At PMQs soft questions extend her reach
160   And later she makes an impassioned speech
To the Tory 1922 probing
Committee – one MP told her to bring
Her own noose – and faces down the tumbrel.
All's well, and it's rumoured the EU will
Offer a UK-wide customs union
And regulatory alignment based on
The single market although this would stop
The UK making free-trade deals on top.
      The Treasury's top mandarin says Brexit
170   Will leave the UK in the red and not permit
A dividend because of the huge cost
Of leaving, all the benefit's been lost.
The French may cripple Calais and British ports.
The PM's struggling with backstop onslaughts
And's cancelled an inner Cabinet meeting
As her new plan's not ready, there's no briefing.

Barnier says a Brexit deal may never
Be reached, and 'no deal' will not deliver
A transition, or peace in Northern Ireland,
180   Or keep the Union together as planned.
It's been *impasse* in Brussels, and ahead
'No deal' fills all with foreboding and dread.

There's a sound of silence in Brussels' sun
Which usually means that work is being done.
A leak from Barnier without May's blessing,
A development after months of scribbling.
At last, a secret Brexit deal: backstop
Has been tweaked and Brussels will allow as a sop
The whole of the UK to stay as a safeguard
190   In a customs union and avoid a hard
Border with Northern Ireland, and's let slip
A future economic partnership
With the EU, with the prospect ahead
Of a Canada-style free-trade deal instead.
There's a two-way-facing, Janus policy.
Regulatory checks on goods can be
Within the market, at shops and factories,
Rather than at the border, and the EU is
Writing an all-UK customs content
200   Into the legally-binding Agreement.
      Barnier's been more flexible, as required
By Merkel and Macron, the deal's transpired
And will be sealed at an EU Council
Meeting in November, with no ill will.
Raab's said Britain should be able to end
The backstop unilaterally and amend.
But Ireland's Taoiseach's said there must be no
End-term for the customs union, no up-and-go.
      Now May presents it to her inner Cabinet,
210   Saying the deal must be signed at a banquet
By the end of November so Parliament can hear

And vote on it before the end of the year.
There are calls to publish legal advice –
Which may say that the Union is the price,
And that a 'temporary' stay within
The customs union means being locked in
And that the country's constitutional
Future's at risk. The Brexiteers rumble
That May'll try to bounce them into accepting
220   A much-fudged divorce settlement tying
The UK to the customs union
Indefinitely and stop the sullen
UK from having its own trade deals. She may say,
"Sign off the deal or face a 'no-deal' mayday."
    The full Cabinet are now invited
To a secret room to read a redrafted
Withdrawal Agreement with the Irish
Backstop missing, on which, it's Barnier's wish,
The UK must now decide. It's been descried
230   The EU will allow a UK-wide
Backstop in return for its agreement
To the EU's demands that its insistent
Fishermen must have access to UK
Waters, but have rejected a proposal by May
That an independent system should oversee
How the UK might leave a temporary
Customs arrangement if the talks collapse.
The ECJ rules on laws like satraps.
    A letter from May to the DUP
240   Has been leaked: the UK-wide backstop she
Wants will have another backstop behind it,
A new border down the Irish Sea will split,
"A backstop to a backstop", new content
That will be in the legally-binding Agreement
Even though May says no divide between
Ulster and Great Britain will ever be seen;
And the DUP, whose deal was with the Tories,

Not with May, who has broken promises,
Is set to vote against in Parliament,
250   Make the Government look less competent.
If the trade talks fail Ulster will be repressed
As a rule-taker from the EU, for the rest
Of the UK will have the Chequers plan.
     The French are preparing for a 'no-deal' pan,
They'll check lorries near Calais more carefully
And choke UK trade with security.
There'll be border gridlock and food hardships.
The UK may have to eat home-grown turnips.
Raab says he hadn't "understood" or weighed
260   The importance of the cross-Channel trade
To the UK economy, and how
Reliant the vulnerable UK is now
On a speedy Dover-Calais crossing.
Ten thousand lorries arrive for checking
At Dover each day and carry seventeen
Per cent of the UK's trade. How could it have been
A surprise to Raab that the UK's most
Important trade gateway is the closest coast
To its most important market? May has sought
270   By a give-away budget to win support
From MPs for her deal, which is better than
'No deal'; otherwise the Cabinet has plan
B: paying eighteen billion pounds until
2021 while following – still –
EU rules, so a new free-trade deal's aligned.
     Jo Johnson, Boris's brother, has resigned
(May's seventh minister to jump ship and appeal),
A Remainer who says the latest deal
Is a terrible mistake as the UK
280   Will cede sovereignty, the biggest give-away
Of sovereignty in modern times, and power
To make its own trade deals or grow and tower
With a deregulated economy's reach

(A betrayal of May's Lancaster-House speech).
The choice is vassalage versus chaos –
French blocking of food and medicine, much loss,
And gridlocked lorries throughout Kent, quite daft.
May's deal's a failure of British statecraft,
He says, on a scale not seen since Suez,
290   And the UK's in a crisis that is
The greatest since the Second World War's schism.
He demands a second referendum.
The two brothers, opposing in affray,
Are now reunited in their dismay.
Jo says voters were made false promises
And given a fake guarantee of riches,
And were lied to. He says the Brexit dream
Is undeliverable as a scheme
(Having left the Ship of Fools), a fantasy.
300   Boris calls the Cabinet to mutiny.
      At the hundredth anniversary of the Great War
May remembers the fallen with awe
And Macron. The once-mighty victor now
Looks feeble, ill-informed and middlebrow.
Millions died so the UK could control
Its laws, and have they been betrayed by a mole?
Forty-eight hours to charter a flotilla
To keep trade flowing in a 'no-deal' rupture,
To stockpile medicines and bring in supplies
310   To keep the country going, short-term buys.
      Forty-eight hours to plan 'no deal', yet sit
At the Lord Mayor's banquet, no mention of Brexit
Save it's now reached the "endgame". May looks pleased
As if keeping a secret and has teased.

The Ship of State's ground to a juddering
Halt. The shuddering engine's stopped, it's drifting.
The crew all shout instructions till they're hoarse.
The captain turns the wheel to stay on course,

But the Ship's now at the mercy of currents
320   And winds, invisible forces and portents,
As it dips and tosses in the troughs of waves,
Adrift. Fearful faces near watery graves.
Seagulls hover and soar, and caw and screech
Above hungry faces, they're out of reach.
Starved and hallucinatory from thirst
The passengers cry out as if they'll burst.
Order has broken down, the crew push in
And shove each other to reach the engine.
There's quite a swell, a curling wave gathers
330   And crashes against the side, the Ship shudders.
The captain's steered the Ship on to the rocks.
They're stuck and tossed and battered as each wave shocks.
Where is the land the mariners promised?
The dream of plenty's faded, and does not exist.

Canto XI
Battles over Withdrawal Agreement

Sing, Muse, of the Withdrawal Agreement,
Of UK-wide customs union dissent
And the backstop the EU insisted on.
Sing of thwarted hopes and of division.
And sing how the Withdrawal Agreement
Was signed off in Brussels but received with discontent
By the MPs in the Commons chamber,
Sing of May's difficulties in Westminster.
    At last, a draft Withdrawal Agreement that
10   Is five hundred-and-eighty-five pages fat
And has taken months to agree in Brussels
In late-night meetings, some in a shambles
Till 3am, to draft a form of words
Acceptable to both sides like a blackbird's
Clear, piping song. Olly Robbins has led
The writing – he's bartered away May's red
Lines – and's refused to take the EU's 'stay'
Proposals back to Cabinet as Barnier
Has refused to stop taking the backstop's side.
20   The Agreement will keep the UK tied
To EU trade policy until an end
Is established by "joint consent", a blend
Meaning the EU has a veto and's forced
The UK to cave in on the talks it sourced.
Has there been a breakthrough, by statecraft?
It's time to show the Cabinet the draft
And start the process of winning their support.
    They arrive in dribs and drabs for the endgame's sport,
And read the text in the 10-Downing-Street
30   Reading-room, where they can chew the backstop's defeat.
May sees ministers individually
To lobby support. A leak to RTE,
It's still the Chequers plan, there's a UK-wide

Customs agreement with regulatory-tied
Checks down the Irish Sea that would split the Union.
There are two backstops: there's a provision
For Northern Ireland to have its own backstop
In relation to the single market and prop
Up a deeper relationship with the Republic;
40   And there's an exit mechanism that seems toxic,
It's not unilateral, the ECJ's in charge.
Can the UK exit the customs union, be at large?
A backstop comes into force if a 'no deal' is flexed
But it may trigger rejection of the text
By Brexiteers and the DUP (who will end
Their confidence-and-supply agreement's stipend).
Dublin will have more say than London in how
Northern Ireland is governed. Dublin now
Has the text, Ulster has not seen it yet.
50   May'll put the text to the full Cabinet
The next day. If it's well received, there can be
An EU summit held as an emergency
In Brussels by the end of November –
Without seeing it Johnson calls it surrender –
And a Meaningful Vote before Christmas, the way ahead.
     The ministers pore over the five-hundred-
And-eighty-five-page text, both hands on cheeks,
And simultaneously (so there are no leaks)
The Ambassadors of the twenty-seven
60   Are shown the same text in Brussels, sullen.
Labour say they'll judge it by their six tests
And as the negotiations have been requests
And so shambolic they were unlikely to be
The right deal for Britain, as all can now see.
The EU say the text's not finalised,
It's "stabilised", not "formalised". (It's despised.)
In a separate release the European
Commission states what 'no deal' would beckon.
This deal could fall apart for lack of assent

70   From Tories and DUP in Parliament.
Do the people want it? They may choose to block.
Do the Cabinet want it? Will May get a shock?
    Judgement Day. At a stormy PMQs, hot
Brexiteer Bone warns May that she is not
Delivering the Brexit people voted for
And is losing the support of many MPs and more
Millions of voters. He is distressed.
She says the deal's in the national interest –
The draft text of the Withdrawal Agreement
80   Based on the hated Chequers plan's content –
And that she'll return with a statement. She's open.
    The Cabinet meet at 2 and talk to 7,
She talks to each minister and hears their price
And they all hear Cox's legal advice.
Eleven ministers oppose the text, a threat,
And so there is no vote in Cabinet.
McVey's aggressive towards May and has bawled.
She's in meltdown, security's nearly called.
She's shouted down by the Chief Whip and Cabinet
90   Secretary for demanding a vote in a fret.
In Westminster anger rages, some say
There'll be a no-confidence vote the next day
And the triggering of a leadership contest
By sending a flurry of letters to request
Changing the deal by getting the PM zapped.
If she is out, the draft text will be scrapped.
Just as flocked geese hear a loud noise and squawk,
Necks up towards the sun, and scare a hawk,
So ministers and MPs raised a din
100   At the loud noise round the Withdrawal Agreement's spin.
She's teetering on the edge of her premiership.
She's got the best deal going, it's a snip,
"The deal she always wanted", but it's not
A proper Brexit, there's a garish blot:
There is no unilateral exit

From the customs union. A Committee will sit
And review the ending of the backstop. Know
There's a painful 'no-deal' Brexit and also
A pointless Brexit that leaves the UK worse off,
110   And satisfies no one, and she may now scoff
And go back to the people for a second
Referendum, and the EU may, hardened,
Make a renewed offer after the shambles.
EU officials are waiting in Brussels
For May to emerge and make a statement
As are the DUP, who are incandescent.
     May walks out of 10 Downing Street and speaks
At a large fluffy microphone. She leaks
That after a five-hour impassioned debate –
120   And many meetings to negotiate –
•   The Cabinet's collectively given its consent
To back the text and move on to her statement.
It's now this deal to take control in the spring
Or 'no deal' or no Brexit, suggesting
That if this deal is voted down there'll be
A second referendum to choose freely
'No deal' or remaining in the EU.
She repeats the deal's in the national interest – her view.
No word that the Cabinet were unanimous.
130   Or that the document on the UK's dubious
Future relationship with the EU, a sketchy
Framework that's only politically,
Not legally, binding, some eight pages,
Has been expanded to twenty – still wishes
Or aspirations, no concrete process.
     In Brussels Barnier speaks of decisive progress.
The deal avoids issues on the Irish borders,
And there'll be EU access to British waters,
In return for UK fish being sold
140   In the EU (on which the UK is cold).
It's a 'take-it-or-leave-it' deal, that's plain.

The EU say it's the final text yet Spain
Will vote against it unless it has a veto
Over Gibraltar's future; but it has no
Veto now, it's qualified majority voting,
Twenty countries must back it at a meeting
On Sunday. But when the UK leaves, Spain will
Have a veto on the free-trade deal, and can grill.
The Withdrawal Agreement and the Political
150   Declaration are closed. The optional
Transition can last until 2022,
Or until the next UK election's due.

The Brexiteers are deeply furious.
The UK is now more precarious,
Far closer to the EU than they'd thought.
Their expectations have been thwarted and are fraught.
They're seeking to vote the deal down and win,
And resignations start to trickle in:
Raab, McVey, Vara, Braverman and an aide.
160   May's statement in the Commons has dismayed,
It's seen as appeasing the EU,
She seems like Chamberlain, clutching a view,
Back from Munich with a paper reprieve.
It's said she's broken promises – to leave
The customs union, to keep the UK
Union together, and break from the ECJ.
These broken promises push Rees-Mogg to request
Why he should not call for a leadership contest –
And he hands a letter to Brady, to press.
170   A far-right *coup* on the leadership's in progress.
But it soon descends into chaos, support's too few.
An interviewer calls it a *Dad's Army coup*,
The Brexiteers have been outplayed with ease,
And May says different things to different MPs –
To Remainers "no deal", to Leavers "no Brexit" –
To corral them into voting for her deal, with such grit.

Asked to replace Raab Gove will not be next
Unless he can renegotiate the text
And an end to the customs union and backstop.
180   He's turned the offer down and is staying on top.
        After a turbulent, tumultuous day
Of turmoil caused by the intransigent way
Of Leavers who desire total victory
So a second referendum's necessary,
May holds a news conference and stands firm.
She says she'll carry on, and many squirm.
The DUP withdraw their confidence-
And-supply arrangement, and so silence
The Government's handling of the Finance Bill.
190   The budget's at risk, May concedes with skill.
She meets the Brexiteers, and says she'll seek
For an alternative for backstop in sleek
New technology, which Brussels will ignore.
She is playing for time in a covert war
To ensure Brady does not have forty-eight letters,
Frantically keeping the DUP partners.
She's in office, but not in power, all feel.
        She says in Parliament that it's *her* deal
Or back to square one: staying in the EU.
200   She says there won't be a better deal to view.
It delivers on the referendum's say,
It ends free movement and the ECJ,
It ends sending money to the EU,
It takes back control of the UK's menu
Of money, laws and borders, fisheries
And common agricultural policies,
And leaves the customs union but protects
Jobs, security and the Union's subjects.
But she may have misunderstood what Leavers mean,
210   She may see Brexit as a need to screen
And reduce immigration, which is why
She's opposed by all who want 'EU, goodbye'.

The Whips say she must wring a concession
From Brussels to get her deal for the nation
To Parliament but she believes that fear
Of 'no deal' will persuade MPs to be clear
And vote her deal through. She has tried to please
All sides, and has ended pleasing none, to appease.

May returns to Brussels on Wednesday for more
220   And is told by Juncker on the thirteenth floor
Of the Berlaymont that the Withdrawal Agreement
Is a closed text and a done deal he'd prevent
From being reopened and amended.
She attempts to give flesh to a free-trade thread
That can remove the backstop and customs union,
That have alienated her party's stubborn,
In the twenty-six-page Political Document
On the future relationship with the intransigent
EU. No trade deal can be negotiated
230   Or signed till the UK's left the EU's homestead.
Spain wants a veto on Gibraltar,
And Germany, Holland and France concur
In demanding fishing access to English waters.
There's no mention of frictionless trade. She confers,
Can a free-trade deal with the EU be written
In two years when it took Canada seven
And Singapore eight years to do their deals?
     Juncker does not reopen, despite her appeals,
The draft Withdrawal Agreement, whose text
240   Has legal force and dictates what happens next:
A transition, the UK's staying firmly
In the customs union in perpetuity
Unless it accepts the terms for departure
The EU dictates. He does not lift the blocker,
"Joint consent", so the UK can be made to wait
Forever in the backstop as a vassal state
("A state held by the will of a superior lord").

He ignores the ministers gathering in discord
To trigger a no-confidence vote in May.
250   And she returns empty-handed and grey.
The draft Political Declaration's agreed
At negotiators' level, and indeed
In principle at political level.
The DUP and Johnson both squabble
And urge a new agreement. May appeals
To the public to pressure their MPs' ideals.
She says the Agreement has a transition, and bites.
It guarantees EU and UK citizens' rights,
A soft Irish border and tariff-free trade,
260   And thirty-nine billion pounds must be paid.
It's legally binding, the UK's locked in,
If 'no deal' is triggered 'backstop' will begin
And turn all UK subjects into fools
Applying EU tariffs and customs rules.
The Declaration must be approved promptly
By each member state unanimously,
So each has a veto over the assent
To the future UK-EU trade agreement.
May's condemned on all sides, she lacks support.
270   The arithmetic for the vote on her deal is fraught.
      May returns to Brussels on Saturday.
It's agreed that any trade deal between the UK
And Gibraltar must be approved by Spain separately,
That the UK and Spain have "co-sovereignty",
The biggest change on Gibraltar for three hundred years.
Cries of "sell-out" are dismissed as mere smears.
      At the summit on Sunday, a sombre,
Serious, sorrowful day in the Europa
Building, the day of the first member state's divorce
280   From Europe's union, the EU leaders endorse
The Withdrawal Agreement in just thirty-eight
Minutes, so short a time to abnegate
Forty-five years. There is no discussion.

The leaders agree in just a few seconds on
A sad divorce, and sign immediately
Because the UK's in dependency
And they don't want May to change her mind and suspend.
Tusk says, "We will remain friends to the end."
Juncker says the British called a halt.
290   He means it is the Brexiteers' fault.
But couldn't he have been more flexible,
And made concessions and been more humble
To Cameron so a win for Remain could be had?
    A border is closing, and it's sad, sad
For when the Nazis ruled all Europe who
Stood alone and came to Europe's rescue
With the US at D-Day, lay down lives for
Europeans as in the First World War?
(Your poet's uncle died at nineteen, shot
300   Down when flying a Bristol Fighter that had got
To photograph German positions in France
On a spying mission for an advance
And was buried in Gavrelle in September
1918, which he'd helped recapture.)
O sad, in 1946 Churchill
Called for a United States of Europe – a thrill –
And planned for the Council of Europe to sit,
Which now endorses the UK's exit.
The UK's leaving its heritage, won
310   By the sacrifice of brave troops who'd outgun,
And it is now as divided as before
The outbreak of Parliament's Civil War,
And just as families were split and some rivals
Fought for Charles' *status quo*, some for Cromwell's
New extremism that did not last a decade,
So now families like the Johnsons are splayed
And fight to remain and to leave, both sides of the clan
Are united in loathing for the Chequers plan.
O sad, sad, it's the first withdrawal to jeers

320   From Europe's togetherness in sixty years.
         At a news conference, without celebration,
      Robbins standing as if at a cremation,
      May says the Agreement ends free movement from shores,
      Brings back control over money and laws,
      And urges MPs to back the Agreement
      In Parliament. She's gambling on a decent
      Trade deal. New countries put down their markers –
      Spain on Gibraltar, France on British waters –
      For wrangling that looks hostile to the UK,
330   And they won't vote for a trade deal if they
      Don't get what they want out of national avarice.
         Macron says the UK must out of justice
      Open its waters to French fishing fleets
      After Brexit or be locked into the feats
      Of a permanent customs union, unfree.
      May says she'll ban French fishing boats if he
      Blackmails her over an EU trade deal then.
      It's like the Cod War all over again,
      When the UK and Iceland fought over fish and the law.
340   Alas, where there's nationalism a war
      Between nation-states isn't far away.
      The EU Commission and Council say
      This is the only Agreement, there's a default position:
      If it's voted down, 'no deal' and no transition.

      The Ship of State's listing, broken in two.
      Above the wind's roaring, captain and crew
      Are battling with the engine-room and wheel
      And try to raise a sail, protect the keel,
      As if the Ship is not stuck on jagged rocks,
350   As if it's not shaken by fierce waves' shocks.
      The passengers are wailing but their cries
      Are lost in the wind's whistling, and the sky's
      A lowering black, a storm is approaching.
      Where is the land of plenty they were heading

Towards, where is the paradise all saw
On the horizon, the inviting shore?
The captain's refloating, eager to find
A better life for all, and he seems blind
To the worse-off plight of the trusting fools
360   Who follow him and obey all the rules.
O if only the Ship had not set sail,
None would be clinging to a sinking rail.

Canto XII
Humiliation

Sing, Muse, how the next Brussels summit ended
In a rebuff for May, who was contradicted.
Sing of the EU's long-term strategy
And the Chequers plan's demise and obsequy.
Sing how lack of concessions was a blow,
Sing of severance, sadness and great sorrow.
Sing, Muse, of the Meaningful Vote and the way
Forward, and the nightmare haunting the UK.
And how May's far right attempted a *coup*

10   That shamed the Brexiteers, who'd not thought things through.
      On Monday in the Commons hostility wears a hood.
Brexiteers want the perfect and have turned on the good,
They prefer an ideal to the reality.
The Agreement's savaged, there's talk of venality,
Of peerages and knighthoods being due.
Trump says it's a good deal for the EU
But it could scupper a US trade deal, his goal.
The UK has not taken back control
But's handed control to the EU without

20   A British presence in Brussels – MPs pout.
What was promised is not in this Agreement's flummery:
A dividend of three-hundred-and-fifty
Million pounds a week on the side of a bus,
And free-trade agreements with all states, in surplus.
May says in Parliament that it's her deal – all frown –
Or 'no deal' or if that is voted down
No Brexit – revoking Article 50.
If there's 'no deal' a recession will be costly:
The Bank of England warns the pound will crash,

30   A million jobs will be lost, there'll be shortage of cash,
A million fewer migrants for less work;
Inflation will soar, interest rates rise in the murk.
House prices will fall by a third, the pound

By a quarter, and growth will be near the ground.
It's forecast that compared with staying in
The EU, the UK would lose within
Fifteen years about a hundred and fifty
Billion pounds if there's 'no deal', and forty
Billion if the Chequers plan is ratified.
40   Why not remain, lose nothing and be satisfied?
        At Argentina's G20 meeting
May wears a necklace of twenty-something
Large red beads that resemble red cherries
'Cherry-picked' from the EU's best goodies.
She flaunts her deal's cherry-picking and blocks
The publishing of legal advice – that shocks –
As it shows the UK will be trapped indefinitely
In a customs union, and barred by backstop, utterly,
From having trade deals. Robbins, who wrote the Agreement,
50   Told her it was "bad for Britain" in a letter he sent,
Having been urged to write it by Barnier.
She's been led into a quagmire, and won't say.
        The Attorney General confirms that the backstop stay
Will be indefinite. The shocked UK
Parliament on a vote decides that ministers
Are in contempt of Parliament's procedures
For withholding the full legal-advice content
And on another vote gives Parliament
Control of Brexit if May's deal is blocked,
60   So there can't be a 'no-deal' exit, it's locked.
May's lost control over her Brexit package
And the MPs now have vast leverage
Over Brexit's next steps. Within an hour,
The three worst defeats of a Prime Minister's power
In the Commons for forty years. The legal advice
Is published the next day and states in precise
Terms the backstop's forever, and the Withdrawal
Agreement is now dead. May has nine loyal
Members of the Cabinet to Downing Street

70   And asks what she should do to avoid defeat.
             She's no idea what to do, but must do something.
       The debate for the Meaningful Vote is in full swing.
       She's expected to lose by more than a hundred,
       There's an *impasse* as the carping Brexiteers hothead:
       The thirty-nine billion pounds given away
       For nothing in return, to their dismay;
       A Political Declaration that's not binding;
       No end to free movement; laws still being
       Made in Europe and judged by the ECJ;
80   Saying the backstop must be stopped or UK
       Bucks stop; and demanding May returns to Brussels
       To refuse to hand over one penny of the oodles
       Of billions till the backstop is ditched. They will choose
       Paradise over reality and confuse.
       Just as in a field a sheep heads towards a hedge
       And soon the flock follow to the field's edge,
       So the MPs headed to the far right
       As if the Withdrawal Agreement filled them with fright.
             The Ship of State is indeed sailed by fools.
90   Our leaders now seem idiots without rules.
       Were voters who followed them any better?
       All wait to hear if the Agreement is over
       And replaced by 'no deal' – disruption at ports
       No drinking-water, bare supermarkets of sorts –
       Or remaining in the EU on less good terms.
       May ploughs on like a character that squirms
       In ignorance of the plot the dramatist knows,
       Advancing the plot without realising she chose
       But not knowing the outcome that's been plotted:
100   That first key Brexiteers resign hothead
       Over the Chequers plan accepted by
       The EU, and that this will have effects and bring nigh
       'No deal', her fall and staying-in, seeds all sown.
       Only at the very end will the outcome be known.
       She ploughs on, knowing the UK will be

Worse off as several generations will see,
Driven by being determined to honour
An outdated referendum now a blur,
And, in self-delusion or deception,
110 With no choice but to ride for her nation
Into the Valley of Death with the six hundred
In the Meaningful Vote on the Agreement that's dead
And then appeal to the EU for better terms.
She may be the most incompetent PM with her squirms
Since Lord North, who lost the American colonies.
She's like Micawber, something will turn up riches.
She's living in a fools' paradise, at ease
As her Ship of State founders in mounting seas.
  A shock. In a necklace of dark and pale blue beads,
120 Having known for weeks there was no support for her leads,
May's halted the debate for a Meaningful Vote
So a hundred-and-sixty-four speeches are a footnote,
In the face of defeat that is three-figure,
And she's deemed discourteous by the Speaker.
She's accused of being "frit" and chaotic.
She's going back to Brussels to seek fire-brick
Legal assurances the backstop will occur
As long as necessary and no longer,
Though the EU and Ireland say nothing can be changed
130 That's been agreed. The Meaningful Vote's rearranged –
Postponed to the new year. The EU'll be discussing
Facilitating the UK's ratifying
But won't renegotiate or back down on
The backstop Ireland wants and as much time's gone
All are prepared for 'no deal'. So the Ship of State's
Captain has shaken hands on withdrawal dates
With the EU, then seen there's no support, just a squeal,
And's seeking assurances on the same deal
That's just been negotiated, which she has said
140 Is the best deal. It's madness, the deal's dead.
It looks as if the Ship's being run by fools.

She's saving her premiership by playing the rules,
By getting through to January like an arch
And then surviving till the end of March
Like Quintus Fabius Maximus Cunctator,
The Delayer, who delayed to survive in war.
    More letters have reached Graham Brady, a no-
Confidence vote looms as she goes to Brussels to slow
Things down and negotiate though Tusk's said no more
150   Negotiations. The deal was done before
The Chequers ambush: May'd present the EU's
Withdrawal Agreement knowing it would lose
Support from her party and Parliament,
But in the process the most truculent
Brexiteers would fall away and allow her –
With the help of the backstop's smokescreen and her adviser –
To steer a soft Brexit through Parliament
And keep the UK in the EU's orbit, present
As a serf state, shorn of all influence and hold
160   (Or better still, creep back into the fold).
That was the plan, but now she has to fight
A no-confidence vote within her party's plight.
Delaying the Meaningful Vote's created
Time for a no-confidence vote to be brought to a head.
May visits Berlin, and sees Merkel lurk
On a red carpet but can't make the car door work.
She can't get out of her car, let alone the EU.
    Forty-eight names have now been received, it's true.
Brady informs the PM, who addresses
170   'The 1922' and promises
To resign by the next election. Votes are counted.
Brady announces: two hundred are said
To have confidence, a hundred-and-seventeen
Do not, she's won the vote and is now seen
As safe for a year from her party. There's been a stay
Of execution but she can't delay
Her fate indefinitely. It's a pyrrhic victory,

She's lost control and's heading for catastrophe.
But the Brexiteers have failed to carry through
180   Their dethroning of May, their bloodless *coup*.
There's seething as well as rejoicing. May's survived
But a hundred and seventeen of her MPs have skived
From her, and there's not the arithmetic to try
And win the Meaningful Vote and ratify
The Withdrawal Agreement, or bring in new
Legislation to leave by March, she can't carry it through.

The day before Brussels' summit in December
Robbins agrees with Serafin and Selmayr,
Tusk's Chief of Staff and Juncker's aide, a text
190   And strategy, that the summit, which may be perplexed,
Will jointly agree the backstop's not desirable
And will only operate for an equable
"Short period" with further assurances
At a summit in mid-January, promises
Of co-operation. The draft Agreement
Is circulated to EU ambassadors, sent
With security marks to prevent leaks, but it
Is leaked before Thursday's EU summit.
    May speaks for seven minutes in the Brussels hotbed,
200   Saying "You can trust me" and asking for a go-ahead
For talks on the jointly-agreed strategy,
But this time she's interrogated for fifty-three
Minutes. Merkel asks several times of the new
Trade relationship, "Exactly what do
You want?" May wants a legally-binding
Assurance the backstop can't be a never-ending
Trap, a legal guarantee in the treaty
That it will have an end date, but she's very
Unspecific as her Cabinet has not
210   Decided and so she cannot get what
She wants through Parliament. She can't explain
What assurances she's seeking and there's strain,

She's accused of wanting the EU to ban
The backstop without putting forward a plan.
She asks for further talks in January.
    The EU leaders refuse as she can't guarantee
She'll get the Withdrawal Agreement into law.
Several say Brexiteers could come back for more
Concessions. May brings up ideas deemed unfit

220   And rejected. She says "Brexit means Brexit"
And exasperates the twenty-seven leaders.
She threatens if they won't be her helpers
She'll lose the vote and crash out to 'no deal'.
She comes across with an unprofessional feel.
    She's put their backs up. When May leaves the room
Ireland, France, Sweden, Spain and Belgium fume
And urge all helpful language should be removed
From the summit conclusions, and all approved.
She asked for assurances, they've deleted, vexed,

230 . The paragraph on assurances in the text
Of the summit conclusions, a clause about
The backstop being temporary's been left out
As a warning to the UK Parliament
And to discourage Brexiteers, make them relent.
There's no breakthrough, Juncker says on TV, sedate,
He'd like clarifications as the "debate"
Is sometimes "nebulous" (cloud-like and hazy,
Vague) and "imprecise" – that's aimed at May, clearly –
And that the British have not read or understood

240   The Agreement, the wording is quite clear and good
And can't be renegotiated as if a hurdle.
It's up to May to get the Withdrawal
Agreement through Parliament, not the EU.
    This summit's been worse for her than even the askew
Salzburg summit that also stoked her anger.
Emotions have run high. In the chamber
May angrily confronts Juncker, "You called me
Nebulous, yes you did." She insists she

Has been "crystal-clear". Juncker spreads his calm
250   By placing a comforting hand on her arm.
To the EU it's incomprehensible
The UK's House of Commons, once a marvel,
Used to be "the Mother of Parliaments"
But now seems a shambles of querulents.
There are small countries (it's said in an EU drawl)
And countries that don't realise they are small.
It's tragic the UK will recede
But the best possible deal has been agreed.
    The Chequers plan led to the Withdrawal
260   Agreement and though there's no chance it'll
Be approved in Parliament, brilliant EU
Minds proposed and worked it, and saw it through.
Just as a brilliant chess Grand Master can see
Ten moves ahead and know where he should be
And just as a brilliant diplomat can project
Ten moves backwards from his goal to effect
A step-by-step progress to his desired end,
So Barnier with help from Robbins would attend
To Ireland, Denmark and Holland, which were regained –
270   All had two referendums and remained –
And plot a scenario that would take May
From the Chequers plan – balancing both sides, a way
That would shake out the extremists, who would fall
(Davis, Johnson, Raab) – to alienating all
And lead to 'deal', 'no deal' or 'no Brexit',
A choice that gravitates to the favourite,
And home in on rejection of the deal
And on fear of 'no deal' and its lack of appeal,
So the only alternative is 'no Brexit',
280   Revoking Article 50 to permit
A pause to sort things out, which will be in vain,
And then as time elapses to remain.
Is not a house bought subject to survey,
And once the facts are known do not all weigh

The actualities, not wishful thinking,
Money out and in, and the travelling?
It's a brilliant piece of dramaturgic skill
With deliberate stymies to achieve standstill.
Just as a dramatist writes out a plot
290   With scenes that lead to what a winner's got
So Barnier and Robbins delivered their goal
Of scheming a hated and imploding sole
Deal that would be rejected by all sides
And leave no time for alternative guides
So the UK could stay in the EU
As had been planned before the Chequers *coup*.

After a tumultuous week with more turmoil
May insists in a press-conference recoil
That clarification on the backstop's themes
300   Is possible in the coming days. She seems
To be stuck on the now-defunct joint Agreement
In the future trade relationship's consent,
But the Withdrawal Agreement can't be edited
And's harsher, and she leaves Brussels empty-handed.
    Now May's in a trap with no escape. In vain
She's proposed the treaty should state a humane
Start date for the new trade deal, not an expiry
Date of the backstop. Her delaying journey
To Brussels achieved nothing, and a third
310   Of her MPs want her gone. And her word
Is not trusted. The EU will not budge
And nor will Parliament, and she must fudge.
There's total stalemate, a complete *impasse*,
And the ways forward are impossible, her *volte-face*
Is the one improbable course that remains,
That's not her deal or 'no deal' with its chains,
The UK shut out of seventy EU
Trade deals: staying in through a revoking *coup*.
    The Meaningful Vote will be in mid-January,

320   And if May's deal is voted down then she
Will bring new proposals to Parliament.
She's accused of running down the clock, hell-bent
On panicking all Tory voters, Corbyn
Tables a motion of no-confidence in
The Prime Minister personally. May sits
Hunched, then walks out. The Brexiteer pirates
And DUP on her side now, she ignores
The no-confidence motion and redraws
Preparations for 'no deal'. Letters are sent

330   To six million businesses to present
What they should do. Three-and-a-half thousand
Troops stand by as the mood's palpably hardened.
High-skilled workers are welcome, low-skilled can stay
For up to a year. Seasonal workers can sway
Agriculture, students can still reside.
There'll be no target to reduce the migrant tide,
And there'll be free movement for seven years. Does May feel
She can scare MPs into voting for her deal?
    Over Christmas all MPs are to reflect:

340   To vote for her deal and keep their jobs, or reject
And lose their jobs. Some wrestle with their conscience:
A people who in living memory ruled an immense
Quarter of the world's population can surely
Govern itself without help from Brussels, fairly.
Foreign-Secretary Hunt has said it's plain
The UK could create a global chain
Of democratic nations ruled freely,
But four hundred MPs are uneasy
At the impending exit with May's deal whereby

350   The UK'd remain with an economic tie
As a satellite of the EU unable to chase
Its own trade deals and losing its fixed place
On the decision-making councils, which seems strange.
They'd not have dreamed of backing such a change
If it weren't for the referendum. They believe

The voters reached the wrong decision, and grieve
As a generation of foolish old men, of fools,
Began a downward decades-long slide that misrules
The UK into a sad decline, and those
360   Who initiated it and recklessly chose
Are already dying out, leaving the rising
Generation of new voters smouldering,
Cut off from a Europe they want to embrace.
It's a British muddle, the MPs grimace:
The EU can't be expected to interfere
In solutions to Britain's problems and its frontier.
There's a feeling that Article 50
Should be revoked or delayed indefinitely.
These Christmas reflections send a chill breeze
370   Into the souls of most Tory MPs.

The mariners are shaken, they have seen
Their dream of settlement seized by a mate who's mean.
They saw a land of plenty across the waves,
A prosperous paradise where none are slaves.
They're stuck on rocks, make pretence of ploughing on,
The captain steers the wheel but the engine's gone.
All want the broken Ship of State to miss
The Scylla of shipwreck and Charybdis
Of returning back home. O what became
380   Of the dream of all the fools? Many passengers blame
Them for basing plenty on a lie. They thought
It would never be delivered as they sought
Influence by positioning themselves without
A plan, for seats on the fools' council and clout.
Their plenty was a fantasy, now most have seen
They will be poor and for some time have been
Heading for a disaster and can only be saved
By returning home, for which most have craved.

Canto XIII
Parliament Seizes Control

Sing, Muse, of defeats of the Government,
Of the Meaningful Vote and of dissent,
Sing of the consequences of delay
And of the nightmare haunting the UK.
And sing of a meeting with the Speaker,
Of how his choice of amendments caused a stir.

    A new year in Parliament and nothing to show
For delaying the Meaningful Vote and the expected blow –
May's forecast to lose by more than two hundred –
10   Save a possible pledge by the EU (that will, it's said,
Lack legal basis) for a trade deal to be done
With the UK by 2021.
There would then be no backstop, and less dissent.
Now another defeat for the Government
In an amendment to the Finance Bill:
A vote to restrict tax-raising powers, that will
Relate to Brexit if there is 'no deal',
A way of throttling 'no deal' that's genteel.
It's Parliament versus the people now,
20   May's deal, which will be voted down, or 'stay in' somehow.

    An amendment in December by Grieve (who
Led calls for a Meaningful Vote to be held, a *coup*)
Established this Vote can be amended by MPs.
The EU Withdrawal Act states that if these
MPs vote against May's deal the Government
Must within twenty-one days make a statement
Setting out how it proposes to proceed.
And now Speaker Bercow (whose job is to plead
For back-benchers, grasping that only MPs
30   Can break the *impasse* that's caused by the squeeze
Between Parliament and the executive)
Allows Grieve to table a subversive
Amendment to the Government's business-

Of-the-House motion on the procedural progress
If May's deal's voted down, that May's statement
Should be brought to the House for its assent
And should be made within three days and an MP
Can attach a rival plan alongside Plan B.
Grieve's amendment's on the order paper, it's been printed.
40   Bercow's ruled the motion can be amended
Although it included the word "forthwith", which means
To MPs "without debate". There are scenes
As he has overruled his clerks' advice.
There's uproar in the Commons, and Bercow's twice
Accused of breaking Parliamentary rules,
Of ignoring a century of precedent. One mewls
That only a minister can amend and harden
A Government's business-of-the-House motion
And timetable, not Grieve, who's a back-bencher.
50   His clerks said it's against a standing order
Of the House, he's overruled them with "Speaker's instruction".
Now all can amend a "forthwith" motion.
    He has changed the rules for an arbitrary goal,
And Parliament has taken back control
From the executive, in what seems a planned *coup*
As if a constitutional lawyer drew
Bercow's attention to reinterpreting
"Forthwith" and "Speaker's instruction" while urging
Grieve to table his amendment in time
60   For the order paper, co-ordinating to chime
Soon after the Christmas recess – it looks contrived
But no doubt both Bercow and Grieve arrived
At the same idea on their own, to build a bridge –
To turn the procedural rules to advantage,
With a people's vote alongside Plan B?
In points of order MPs – all Tory –
Challenge Bercow's interpreted dissent.
Bercow says if he always went by precedent
There'd be no change and he's now setting a new

70   Precedent. The amendment is voted on. All queue.
           The tellers call the votes: there are gasps that say
           Grieve's amendment has triumphed, there's dismay.
           The Commons' greater control of the Government
           Will curtail May's tendency to make frequent
           Delaying returns to beg the EU
           For more concessions. As if acting on cue
           The EU says that 'no deal' would mean the UK'd
           Revert to WTO rules on trade
           And face the EU's tariffs, which would mean
80   The price of goods would rise as has been foreseen.
           It's just been revealed that Bercow met Grieve
           In his grace-and-favour apartment on the eve
           Of the furore, on Tuesday evening, to hook
           Up just hours before he tore up the rule book
           To allow Grieve to table an amendment
           To wrest control from the PM and Government.
           And now it's revealed that Smith, Chief Whip, has told May
           That in the Commons cloakroom on Thursday –
           Purple ribbons on coat-hangers for MPs
90   To hang their swords, where overcoats now squeeze –
           He overheard, unseen, "a senior Tory
           Back-bencher" discussing a plan, excitedly,
           For Parliament to seize control of the business
           Of the Government and of the Brexit process
           By allowing MPs to propose and draw
           Up Commons business so they can pass a law
           To suspend or overturn Article 50 – what?
           Letwin is allegedly behind the plot.
           Your poet met Letwin at a dinner in
100   2003 when he had just been
           Made Shadow Chancellor, and asked him "Will you still
           Do your morning job?" – he worked for Rothschilds till
           Noon – and he said, "Yes, it's staying in touch with the real
           World, MPs should have knowledge of banking, a good feel."
           So Rothschilds who own or control the central banks

Of most of the UN countries and their think-tanks
Including those in France and the UK
Are behind Barnier and Letwin, to dethrone May,
And behind the collusion between Grieve and Bercow –
110   It's a Rothschilds lawyer's *coup* that is now go?
Your poet was right to detect a British *coup*,
Speaker and saboteurs plotting a rescue.
All had a heroic aim, to save the day
From an imploding Government that's lost its way.
In a constitutional struggle between three
Sectors – voters, Government and MPs – key
Figures in the EU and UK Establishment
Have crushed those who want independence and self-government.

The imperial reach of the EU has stayed strong
120   And France and Germany herald in a long
Era of integration with shared foreign,
Defence and economic policies, and army, in
A 'twinning' that will be a prototype for
The European Union's future law,
A stepping-stone to a distant World State.
Will the UK now be a part of this fate
After it's revoked Article 50?
Hunt says if May's deal's voted down it's likely
Brexit won't happen – and the mood will turn sour,
130   Will an election bring Labour to power
And see such integration through? All MPs
Wait to hear with considerable unease,
Will there be a vote of no-confidence in May
After the deal is voted down, or a delay
Until after Plan B? And then a new
Way forward? And then...? History gives a clue.
    Under the Law of History no nation
Can 'walk out' of its civilisation.
The European civilisation's now in
140   A union stage, so the EU's sovereign.

When the union decays it will break up and fragment
To a group of states with a central government
But internal independence, like the USSR:
A federation, protected from afar,
Maintaining flowing trade and brisk business.
To go from union to self-government's reckless.
The European civilisation's been aligned
With the British Isles since the Roman Empire declined.
Ireland, Holland and Denmark all came near
150   To walking out but remained within its frontier.
The UK can't walk out of its own civilisation
And will remain despite humiliation.
So says the Law of History, which is always right.
Your poet speaks with oracular insight.

     In the gathering storm the Tories are split and reel,
Twelve ex-ministers urge voting down May's deal,
A Whip resigns, opposed to the deal too.
May makes her statement on leaving the EU.
She reads a letter from Tusk and Juncker,
160   And another from Cox, which say that their further
Assurances have legal force and glaze
In international law, and she talks of ways
To make sure backstop does not happen: speed
Up the Political Declaration, get agreed
A trade deal before the backstop kicks in.
She pleads with all MPs to support her spin.
But the EU has not made any recent
Concessions on the Withdrawal Agreement
As if they give the Brexiteers an inch
170   They'll take a mile, they'll pinch and pinch and pinch.
There are no legally-binding assurances.
Corbyn and the SNP leader, 'bullies',
Say the letters don't take them any further.
There's a fractious mood, it's not going well for her.
There's not enough to meet the demands made
By the Brexiteers and the DUP's brigade.

She speaks of what history will say, of the prize.
There's now talk of cross-party compromise
And an amendment to pass a law to deter,
180   Indeed rule out, a 'no deal' – the Paymaster-
General has been filmed carrying a 'no-deal'
List: "No food, no Channel Tunnel." All squeal.
      On College Green a tolling bell, crowds sway.
EU flags flutter on a historic day.
The Lords, Scots' Parliament, Welsh Assembly
Have all voted her deal down heavily.
Inside the chamber with theatrical voice
The Attorney General, in an hour of choice
Ciceronian oratory, waving his arms, brazen,
190   Declaims, "What are you playing at, you are not children
In the playground, you are legislators." MPs'
Time is being used up, there is unease.
There are huge misgivings in every quarter, it's said
It's a fantasy there can be quick trade deals, there's dread
That all parts of the UK will be poorer
Than under the *status quo*, before the rupture,
When the EU funded regions' integrating.
Corbyn speaks and finally May, wearing
Silver beads all the same, just one colour,
200   Saying her plan's silver and all will follow her.
Just as a herd of swine are panicked by
A man waving his arms and his loud cry,
And following their leader all stampede
Over a cliff on to rocks below, indeed
A wrong choice for their cause, so most MPs
Stampede into the Noes lobby like plungees.
      At last the storm breaks. Now the vote's astir.
Four tellers stand and bow to the Speaker.
There are gasps and jeers of astonishment.
210   May's deal's been rejected, she's lost – she's bent –
By two hundred-and-thirty votes, easily
The biggest defeat in Parliament's history –

In the history of British democracy – and has burst
Upon Westminster and plunged it into its worst
Crisis since the Second World War, it may
Have seismic consequences – a Corbyn stay
In number ten and an eventual split
In the Tory party that may then submit;
And the future of the country now looks glum.
220   The once pragmatic Brexiteers have become
Reckless zealots: Davis, Johnson and a few
Other mutinous members of the crew
Have crashed the very Ship of State they sing
On to submerged rocks, and it's now listing.

May sits in shock reflecting on 'no deal',
With no hope, no clue, no confidence, no feel.
She's stunned and rises to the dispatch-box and baulks.
She speaks, composed, saying she will hold talks
To see what will have support from the House, its line,
230   A cross-party compromise. She does not resign
Despite her apparent failure and loss of grip
In strategy, tactics and leadership.
She still hopes to tweak her deal with new "things".
The EU's already said there'll be no meetings,
No concessions on her deal will have consent.
They will not reopen the Withdrawal Agreement.
They call for a new plan and don't conceal
They're stepping up arrangements for 'no deal'.
The UK must say what it wants, like choosing sweets.
240   Barnier's work has been rejected. Tusk tweets:
"Who in the UK will have the courage to say
What the only positive solution is?" – to stay.
(Only a court poet or Shakespearian fool
Can blurt "stay in the EU" without ridicule.)
    Next day Corbyn's no-confidence vote is lost
By nineteen votes as an election would cost
Some Tory MPs their seats so the *crème de la crème*

Hold their noses and vote for the PM.
Wearing a silver chain round her neck, again,
250   Subliminally saying "They're trying to chain
Me", she calls for talks with all parties that day.
(There's no Plan B, just re-dressing Plan A.)
All agree with the conditions: she must end
Her red lines and be prepared to extend
Article 50, hold a people's vote
Or have a customs union, they're at her throat.
Corbyn will not attend until 'no deal'
Is ruled out so he can dither and appeal.
      It looks as if the Chequers plan has worked.
260   It's served its purpose, hogged the limelight, lurked
And crowded out, and blocked, all other deals –
Canada and Norway – and seen off *Spiels*.
It was designed to fail, and has done its job.
It has left the UK without a deal, under mob
Rule, the punishment for leaving that the EU
Wanted, it's taught all UK voters a true
Lesson: Brexit's undeliverable and shunned.
It has seen off Brexit. Still shocked and stunned,
May does not realise this, she does not grasp
270   She's been set up to fail, to loosen her clasp,
That this rejection was the Chequers goal.
May looks a character playing out her role
Of strategy and tactics as a leader should
In a plot whose outcome she hasn't understood.
Ahead is a prolonged period of chaos
As she tries to show the EU she's the boss.
      At Chequers May sets up a conference call
With the Cabinet on the next step, and all
Discuss the plot to outlaw a 'no deal',
280   Parliament's seizing control to make her kneel.
Now in the Commons she makes a statement
On her Plan B, which amounts to confident
Talking and a visit to the EU's top

Three to ask for the removal of the backstop.
Robbins undermines the idea before it's announced,
He texts Hammond that Brussels will not be bounced
Into reopening the Withdrawal Agreement
To change the backstop. The Vice-President
Of the European Parliament rejects
290   Her Plan B before it's announced and corrects.

The mariners are stuck with no land now,
Their dream of plenty has been wrecked somehow.
The Ship of State looks lost, the mutinous crew
Stands by to lynch the captain, mount a *coup*.
The plenty the extremists sought has gone,
It was a fantasy, an illusion.

Canto XIV
On a Unicorn to Brussels

Sing, Muse, of May's Plan B, backstop dissent
And how she sought a mandate from Parliament
To return to Brussels and try to reopen again
The Withdrawal Agreement, and the EU's disdain.
Sing of Parliament's wresting back control
And of history and the European soul.
Sing of the European civilisation
That enfolds each European nation.
     May wants to remove the backstop from the Withdrawal
10   Treaty, and prevent a hard-border meddle,
By other means. What she says is vague, a fudge,
And the EU and Irish Government will not budge.
She seems unrealistic and obstinate
In denial of reality and obdurate.
She won't call other parties to the rescue
As they have not enough votes to get her deal through,
But she'll seek support from her own party fast –
The only way she can get her deal passed –
For an idea the EU's already rejected.
20   The DUP would support her as expected
If the backstop has a three-year sunset clause.
     May says she'll be talking – playing for time, on pause.
She will not stop 'no deal' by revoking
Article 50, Plan B is dithering
And wooing her party's Eurosceptics
For short-term survival instead of a long-term fix:
Breaking with the ERG. Corbyn has his say:
It's the end of hibernation, groundhog day
When a groundhog leaves its hole and if it sees
30   Its shadow, goes back underground in unease.
He's saying she's hidden from the Commons' clime
And's now made hollow statements to buy time.
She's going through the motions to blame the EU,

Running down the clock to a 'no-deal' *coup.*
    Under 'no deal' there would be a big fall
In cross-border trade. The Border Force say all
The UK trade through Dover will nose-dive,
Reduced to between thirteen and twenty-five
Per cent of current capacity in the first
40   Six months of 'no deal', a fall by (at worst)
Seventy-five to eighty-seven per cent,
And the food consortium warns of imminent
Food shortages if there's no deal, when lorries
Will back up on the M20 for ages
And cancer patients can't get their drugs, and there'll be
Disruption to flights and security –
And all this at a time when the WTO
And global trade's unravelling and slow.
Whitehall plans to declare a state of 'war'
50   If there's 'no deal' and impose martial law
To stop civil disobedience with curfews,
Travel bans, armed troops in the streets: bad news.
It's beginning to dawn that there has been
A colossal act of self-harm to the UK scene.
    The Queen has urged her subjects to speak well
Of others and respect different views, not yell;
To come together to seek common ground
And never lose sight of the bigger picture – that's sound –
So the UK can *be* a *united* kingdom.
60   She's head of a United Kingdom that's bedlam
And looks for unity in division.
Some say "common ground" does not mean union
(What's common to foes) but May's deal accepted,
That Downing Street was behind what she said.
    May needs a majority to show the EU
She can get a revised backstopless deal through
Parliament. Brady wants May's deal to be rewrapped
And approved with the backstop being scrapped.
His amendment, supported by May, is being whipped.

70 At a meeting Johnson's confronted her and quipped,
  "What do *you* want, what will this amendment achieve?"
  He has flung down his gauntlet, and May's made him believe
  To nods from the assembled MPs who clap.
  Now Johnson says May is fighting to scrap
  The backstop through a binding legal change.
   The EU says there can be no change – that's strange! –
  To the Withdrawal Agreement. Barnier
  Has rebuffed May's wish to end the backstop's day
  As the cost of hurting the single market
80 Is higher than the cost of a 'no-deal' Brexit.
  He says his job was to make the deal "so hard
  On the British they'll end up wanting to discard
  Brexit, and preferring to stay". He's caused pain,
  But it can't be denied he's advanced 'no deal' again.
   A day of twists and turns with flurries of snow.
  May tells Cabinet that she will now go
  And ask Brussels to reopen the Withdrawal
  Agreement and have a legally-binding removal
  Of the backstop, which will be replaced by
90 "Alternative arrangements", an idea – sigh –
  That's already been rejected by the EU,
  A phrase that's woefully vague, and empty too,
  But possibly meaning a legal codicil
  Attached to the Withdrawal Agreement as to a will
  Which she (perhaps deludedly) hopes will be
  A way forward to harmonious amity.
   Speaking with a silver chain round her neck –
  Suggesting she's chained by her crew to the deck,
  Her party's right wing – and waffling for an hour,
100 She repeats this in Parliament, looking sour.
  There will not be a Meaningful Vote now but, oh dear,
  She's telling the EU what the House wants to hear.
  She wants a mandate to take and grapple
  With the EU, says if there's no Withdrawal
  Agreement ratified – it's now urgent –

Within two weeks she will make a statement.
　　Legal changes to the Withdrawal Agreement
Which can't be changed under treaty law – she's hell-bent,
It's fantasy politics. On this Ship of Fools
110　The captain appeals to the crew that's chewing the rules
To reverse the course she has agreed on advice,
As she sails grimly 'towards' the paradise
The fools behind her believe can still be reached.
Is she zig-zagging? Will her hull be breached?
Who knows. No one has the slightest notion.
The fools sail backwards, in reverse direction.
　　Seven amendments, the MPs have their hour,
All designed to give Parliament more power.
Five are defeated, including one to extend
120　Article 50, but now the MPs contend:
They reject leaving the EU without a deal,
It's not legally binding but can still appeal.
Brady's amendment to dump backstop is run.
The vote's greeted with wild cheering, it's won.
　　Tusk texts, speaking for the twenty-seven,
That the Withdrawal Agreement can't reopen.
The backstop should be even more supreme
So Parliament can't vote in a looser scheme.
The shenanigans in the UK have sent
130　A message: the EU can't trust Parliament.
It seems an Agreement that took years to reach
Has been overturned by the PM in one speech,
Leaving the UK, and Robbins who devised
It, back at square one, utterly compromised.
The EU leaders are irritated with May
And doubt her deal will get through on Valentine's Day.

May's riding a unicorn to Brussels on
A fool's errand with Robbins, Cox, Lidington
And Barclay unless there can be some legal consent
140　Alongside the Withdrawal Agreement:

Technology not yet invented, a time limit
Or a means of unilateral exit
From the backstop, which have all already
Been rejected by the EU and ERG.
It's wishful thinking to believe the EU
Will blink first as a 'no deal' becomes due.
    May's visit will say she's trying but's been blocked,
So she can blame the EU when she's locked
Out of her deal, which won't be ratified,
150   And for her deal-to-'no-deal' downward slide.
An election's planned for June the sixth, and her
Tories are eight points ahead of Labour,
And her fool's errand will play handsomely
In her election narrative, in which she
Is a hard-fighting victim of EU intransigence
Even though she rode a unicorn through common sense.
Political parties have one sole aim:
To win votes and elections with policies that tame.
Parties exist for power, not for the best
160   Interests of humankind, that is oppressed.
    The EU's stepped up planning for 'no deal',
It's asset-stripping the UK piecemeal.
Juncker says the EU will sue for the thirty-nine
Billion pounds or get it somehow, all will be fine.
A European-Council document calls
Gibraltar a "British colony", and appals
As it's an integral part of the UK.
It's an attempt to steal Gibraltar away
With Northern Ireland and new car designs.
170   The EU are buying shares in UK airlines,
At bargain prices, funded from Rothschilds' banks
Which seek to make a killing on Brexit's flanks.
    Perhaps all Brexit is a Rothschilds' scam
To drive down UK assets to a low sham
And hold them while they rise to new riches.
They will lend to relocating companies

And make a profit of trillions before March
When they'll want the UK back under the EU's arch –
Just as they sent a horseman to London to spread
180   A rumour that the British had been defeated
At the Battle of Waterloo and bought the Bank
Of England's fallen shares, which rose to outflank
All when a new horseman announced Waterloo was won.
They now control (bar three) all central banks under the sun.
     May's finished. Her execution's fixed, she'll fail,
But like Scheherazade she spins a tale
To postpone it until all see what she's promised,
"Alternative arrangements" that don't exist.
She madly dismantles the policy she's devised,
190   Procrastinates, delaying her fate, despised.
She's survived so far as there's no successor.
Boris Johnson's unsuitable to succeed her.
He's thrown seventy pages in a garage bin
Which were found by a passer-by who sent them in
To *The Sunday Mirror*. They revile May's deal
"As ridiculous", a "historic mistake", and squeal:
"No deal does not mean crashing out; it can mean
We are getting it right." No, 'no deal' brings, all have seen,
A hard Irish border, and this binning
200   Is a reckless, careless, thoughtless, foolish thing.
     May goes to Northern Ireland and makes a speech.
She says Parliament has voted – stop! I screech –
To "make changes" to the backstop, meaning some tweaks
By the Attorney General, but her last week's
Words were that the backstop should be "replaced"
By "alternative arrangements", which means (when faced)
"Replaced", not "changed"; and the DUP squabble.
She's asked if she's guilty of betrayal
Of Ulster, having U-turned on backstop,
210   And what she'll ask for when she visits Europe.
She does not answer, her visit's not gone well.
She's saying one thing to one side and will tell

The opposite to the other, but both can hear
And know there's double-dealing, that is clear.
All call for clarity to replace opaque,
Deliberate ambiguity that can fake
So a 'harmless' phrase can both reassure and ban.
And underneath it's Brexit without a plan.

A seething Tusk denounces all who deceive
220   After hearing unruly voices clamouring to leave
In France, Greece, Italy and Austria.
He says, standing beside Ireland's leader
And fed up with the UK's prolonged farewell:
"I've been wondering what that special place in Hell
Looks like, for those who promoted Brexit
Without even a sketch of a plan of how to carry it
Out safely." All liars have searing skin
In "the lake burning with fire and brimstone" in
The Book of Revelation. In what circle
230   Of Dante's Hell will the Brexiteer rabble
Deceive with false promises? Surely the eighth, for
Fraudsters who broke the electoral law
And practised sorcery, is not that where all
Who worked on the Withdrawal Agreement will fall
After heading down the steps, to negotiate
Without end or success, with an endless wait,
Free-trade deals with Heaven? They made – conjured –
False promises that could not be delivered
And this deadlock's the result of their mis-sell.
240   Tusk wants all Eurosceptics to roast in Hell.
     Verhofstadt replies. "I doubt Lucifer
Will welcome them, after what they did to stir
Britain they'd manage to divide Hell," he sneers,
And also says the leading Brexiteers
Are like the leaders of the French Revolution –
Gove's like Brissot, Boris Johnson Danton,
Rees-Mogg Robespierre – who, as was not foreseen,

The public turned against and sent to the guillotine.
They'll be voted out, that's how the tumbrel's now used.
250   All Hell has broken loose, Tusk is accused
Of insulting the British going to Brussels
The next day to save all from a 'no-deal' shambles.
      The omens for May's visit to Brussels are bad.
Both sides have entrenched positions that are mad.
In Brussels May takes Tusk to task for his
Inappropriate language, but hers is
No better as she has nothing new to present
And her plans to change the Withdrawal Agreement
Are rejected yet again, it can't be reopened.
260   She's told by Tusk that Corbyn's plan to commend
A customs union's the way out of the deadlock:
A permanent UK-wide union that will shock,
Aligning with the EU's single market and closely
With its workers' rights, agencies and security.
      Tusk's sided against the divided Tory hazard,
He's siding with Labour as a way forward,
Driving the Commons towards Labour's notion
Of a permanent customs union
To avoid the chaos of 'no deal' and swiftly
270   Protect the jobs in the car industry.
Now it transpires the Transport Secretary
In the event of a 'no deal' has cavalierly
Contracted a ferry company with no ships to lend
As reserve ferries between Ramsgate and Ostend,
An act of immense foolishness. Tusk's told May
That her Opposition party has more to say
And a better plan than she has. She'll parley
With Juncker by the end of February
(Kicking the can further down the road). Stubborn
280   May rejects Labour's customs union.
      O nation, things are getting worse daily.
The UK's suffering in Purgatory.
Forty trade deals with seventy-one countries

Have not been agreed, and their amount is
Just twelve per cent of the UK's global trade.
There is no Brexit arrangement that does not downgrade
And contract the UK economy that's now growing
At its slowest rate for nine years, since the banking
Crisis, there will be no Brexit dividend.
290   Recession's rising like a fog at the end
Of an era of forty-six years of a prosperous quest.
The best deal's to stay in, why settle for second best?

There are rumours that the Ship of State is wrecked,
That plenty, which promised so much, has been checked,
Its wreckage strewn across the calming sea;
That the Ship of Fools hit rocks and has shed *débris*;
That crew jumped overboard and are feared lost;
That passengers cling to driftwood, count the cost
And hope to be rescued. Some report anguished cries.
300   Too late many realise they've believed lies.
What happened to the bright new future they
Were heading towards, now taken away?
What happened to their dream of a perfect state?
It's now a mirage that lured some to their fate.
What happened to the trust put in their crew
Now the Ship seems sunk and survivors are few?
But hold, these rumours are based on what's been seen
On a hallucinatory and febrile screen
In a delirious and indignant head.
310   The Ship of State's just stuck, mutiny's dead.

Canto XV
Wreck of a Dream

Sing, Muse, how Parliament voted against 'no deal',
And how wave after wave battered the UK's keel.
Sing of the wreck of Brexit and discontent
And the outcome of the Withdrawal Agreement.
    Now May tells Parliament it has taken two
Weeks to arrange new talks with the EU,
And she needs another two weeks to attend meetings
And then she'll make a statement on amendings
By the end of February, still running down the clock.
She's in a game of brinkmanship, to shock
Europe and the Eurosceptics into blinking,
She's blackmailing all with the threat of 'no deal', gambling
Recklessly with lives and opportunities
And with the UK's trading companies
Which are relocating to Europe and afar.
Robbins is overheard in his Brussels hotel bar
Saying the Brexiteers will face backing (though angry)
May's deal or extending Article 50,
Delaying Brexit for several years rather than
Allowing a 'no-deal' exit without a plan.
    Valentine's Day, and a symbolic vote
In Parliament to remove 'no deal', send a note
To Brussels that there's credible support
As evidence-provision, which is also fraught:
For the furious Brexiteers see it as not far
Removed from Robbins' blurt in the Brussels' bar.
Valentine's Day – will votes be like Valentine cards?
No chance from the seething Brexiteer Life Guards –
A Valentine's Day massacre and nose-dive,
A Government defeat, by forty-five
Because May's extremists don't want 'no deal' removed
As the people voted to leave, 'no deal' was approved,
And now 'no deal' will make that possible –

But did they vote to lose their jobs and stumble?
MPs have voted down the very same
Position they voted for when more tame.
Cash cites Orwell's 'double-think', an adept
Mental capacity that can accept
Two contrary opinions at the same time
40   Without contradiction – May's paradigm
That one can be in and out of the EU
At the same time without this not being true.
(And your poet who holds quite sincerely
All opposites are reconciled in harmony,
$+A + -A =$ zero,
Recognises her thinking as Zen yes-and-no.)
    This vote has left her Brussels mission dead,
And half-killed the legally-binding vote ahead.
She's pandering to her far right, won't face it down,
50   And fobs off with slippery answers and a frown.
A revolution's brewing in the countryside,
Hundreds seize associations far and wide
And seek to deselect all who are Remain –
Far-right and -left momentums purge the sane.
The talks are still in *impasse* despite squabbles.
Tusk still awaits realistic proposals.
Barnier says the vote shows that May's exit
Strategy has failed, no concessions will commit
Or satisfy the insatiable MPs.
60   The EU's running down the clock with ease
To the March summit when there'll be a victory shout.
They'll not flinch and will watch a crashing-out
Or agree a year's extension to keep the UK.
A 'no deal' now looks likely, or a delay.
    Now May has sent a letter to all Tory
MPs, calling for 'double-think' unity,
Saying she's determined to get legally-binding
Changes to the backstop and prevent 'no deal', reconciling.
She's avoided choosing between two wings that don't chime,

70   Delaying to stay in office, but now the time
To choose is looming, both sides can turn against her
And she's facing execution if she doesn't deliver.
Cox meets Barnier to discuss new tweaks that would ease
The backstop clause and reassure MPs.
Juncker tells a German paper in a tease
Brexit's "like being before the courts or on high seas:
We're in God's hands, and we can never be sure
When God will take the matter in hand." He's obscure,
But may God intervene on the EU's side

80   And save May's deal so it is ratified?
      At Sharm el Sheikh May says a deal's within reach
And postpones the next Meaningful Vote till her speech
On the twelfth of March as there is no progress
On toughening the backstop, to her distress.
EU leaders say it's likely instead
That Article 50 will be extended.
Labour says if its customs union's lost
It will back a people's vote – at what cost?
      Back from Sharm May's overruled by her Cabinet,

90   Fifteen ministers revolt, say they'll resign, a threat.
She reluctantly makes a statement she'll adopt.
She says the UK and EU have developed
A workstream to discuss alternative
Arrangements to the backstop, and she'll give
A vote on her deal on the twelfth of March, and there may,
If it's voted down, be a vote on 'no deal' the next day,
And if that's voted down, a vote on extending
Article 50 the day after – to stop the 'revolting'.
(And standing with the Home Secretary among flasks

100   In the Red Lion's Cabinet room, your poet asks,
"Was there a revolt in Cabinet this morning?"
Javid says, "I wouldn't say 'A revolt'", staring
Inscrutably like the Man in the Moon,
And your poet knew that May will be out soon.)
      Now there's news Cox has abandoned trying to fudge

A limit to the backstop as the EU won't budge,
After four hours of talks Cox has walked away.
Barnier's asked for a new plan the next day.
In vain May's bribed pro-Brexit Labour MPs
110   With a billion pounds for their towns, to vote for her deal, please.
She won't lead her party in three years, she's made a vow;
But she could lead it in a snap election now –
Which looms as ten MPs who've resigned design
And found a centre party that can align
All middle-ground voters and get the UK
Out of the Brexit mess with a people's say
And rid it of extreme right who seek 'no deal'
And extreme left who seek a Marxist commonweal.
The choice could be on June the sixth, D-Day, for
120   Its undertones of hostility and war.

At last the Meaningful Vote, and May is hoarse
From scolding ministers, arguing with force,
Reading a lesson in Westminster Abbey
About all the members of the body –
Hands, feet – not rebelling against the whole,
(1 *Corinthians*), then dashing to Strasbourg to enrol
Juncker – who has rejected Cox's loud
Arguing the backstop should dissolve like a cloud,
And offered what in Egypt he said he'd give,
130   Arbitration, a 'joint interpretative
Instrument' legally binding but separate
From the Withdrawal Agreement with no bit,
Not one word, changed from when it was signed off
Back in November – and then, with a dreadful cough,
Being up most of the night, till in mid-morning
Cox has said in writing with much preening
That the legal risk's unchanged, there is no doubt
The UK can't leave the backstop. She's tired out,
She speaks in a husky whisper with a sore throat,
140   With seven large 'shells' round her neck which denote

The seven factions that weigh her down and displease,
In red to appeal for votes from Labour MPs.
There's deal fever, rumours she'll get it through.
But now the vote, crowds throng the lobbies and queue.
    Silence, numbers are read, loud jeers consign.
She's lost again, by a hundred-and-forty-nine.
She says in a hoarse whisper, in a riposte,
There'll be a free vote on 'no-deal', which will be lost,
Dismaying the extremists who have disgraced
150   Her, and that there are now choices that must be faced:
Revoking Article 50, a second
Referendum or a deal that will correspond
And there won't be an extension unless
The EU accepts it will advance progress.
May looks broken, PM in name only,
An enfeebled figure with no authority.
She seems to have lost control of the Brexit blur
And many sense she has to go. After
Clinging to power with a Cunctator's delay
160   She's run out of time, her deal's a mayday.
Just as a song thrush sings a repetitive song
That is heard above the garden birds all day long
But then falls silent and a croak is heard,
So May's repeatings were now a croak, and blurred.
    Next day two votes on 'no deal'. The first appeal
Supports not leaving the EU without a deal,
Ever. A roar, it's lost by four, but is not
Legally binding. The next rejects, gets shot
Of, 'no deal' in any circumstances. A roar and a threat,
170   It's lost by fifty-three. Thirteen Cabinet
Ministers have not supported May despite
Being whipped, there has been a mass revolt. It's right,
May's lost control of her ministers, she'll fall,
It's a dying administration, a free-for-all.
It's the wreck of hard Brexit, some scream
Within at the wreck of their long-held dream.

'No deal', the extremists' utopian dream, has gone.
In a croaky voice May says the default position
Is that the UK will leave without a deal
180   Unless her deal gets passed. More votes repeal:
A managed 'no deal', the Malthouse amendment,
Is lost by two hundred-and-ten, to dissent.
     Now power resides in Parliament, May's power
Is ebbing away, all she can do is glower.
Collective responsibility's broken down though
The EU says, "Agree what you want, let us know."
The MPs know what they don't want, not what they do.
May says there should be a third Meaningful Vote (a *coup*)
In a last desperate roll of the dice next Tuesday.
190   MPs should back her or risk a lengthy delay
To Brexit, a long extension those who fought
For Brexit can't accept, Brexit's on life-support,
And Johnson and Rees-Mogg face voting to select
"A vassal state", or Brexit will be completely wrecked.
     Next day votes on extending Article 50.
The Government wins four votes, one by only
Two and one (agreeing to extend) by
Two hundred-and-eleven. There's a sigh
Of relief but it's humiliating too
200   As the UK's requesting a delay in leaving the EU.
As a third Meaningful Vote looms, all May's MPs
Who voted against have been rung and told, "Please
Vote for her deal so we just extend for three
Months, or else it's two years and perhaps we stay in, see?"
     A bombshell, without notice the Speaker takes aim
And rules the Government can't resubmit the same,
Or substantially the same, proposition
In the same Parliamentary session
As it's against the rules of the House as shown
210   In a 1604 precedent that's been known
And actively used since then. There must now be
A new deal. The Speaker has outfoxed May. She

Warned her party that if her deal was voted down
There would be a crisis, and now all frown
In Cabinet as her deal looks set for a fall,
Doomed for the scrap heap, and there may be no Brexit at all.
    Now May is writing to Tusk to request
An extension for three months in which she can wrest
Control from the Speaker with new stuff she can plead
220   Changes her deal so a third Meaningful Vote's agreed.
But the EU's bound the Withdrawal Agreement
In beautiful binding ("done") and it won't relent.
There must be a clear reason to extend,
One that's useful to the EU and will end
The chaos, there must be a plan, a condition
(Ideally a second referendum or an election).
    The European Commission says the UK
Must leave the EU by the twenty-second of May
Or agree to a longer extension
230   And take part in the European election.
Tusk says a short extension's only possible
If the Withdrawal Agreement wins approval.
The EU leaders are exasperated,
They're filled with incredulity and frustrated,
See a collapse in confidence that may revoke,
And a PM whose chaos is a global joke
And they are preparing for a change of leader,
And they don't want the UK acting as a spoiler
As they press ahead with their integration.
240   There's a crisis in the UK's constitution:
A democratically-elected Parliament
Would stay, and a national democratic vote's in dissent.
Like the Hotel California, the EU's all receive:
You can check out any time you like but you can never leave.

A thousand wasted days, and a statement from
May in Downing Street, lobbed like a bomb.
She stands behind a lectern ill at ease

And says the public's had enough and agrees,
She blames MPs for her delay, and perhaps the moon.
250   She will not delay Brexit beyond June.
      She's an inveterate procrastinator,
She deals in delays like a heartbreaker.
She's broken her promise, expressed repeatedly,
To leave in March, but there's no apology.
She's with the people against Parliament,
And the MPs who must give her their assent.
She threatens if her deal's not passed she'll leave
With 'no deal', but there may be no reprieve.
She has enraged fifty Labour MPs
260   Who've dropped plans to back her deal and appease.
The Chief Whip calls her statement appalling,
It's wrecked his delicate negotiating.
The UK's humiliated, it recklessly
Voted to restore Parliamentary sovereignty,
And now Parliament doesn't know what it's doing.
No one knows what's happening, and the world's laughing.
      In Brussels May speaks to the twenty-seven
EU leaders in a long presentation
Lasting forty-five minutes and is asked several
270   Times what will happen if there's no approval
For her deal and why she so wants to prime
An extension beyond playing for time.
She does not answer, but spreads her hands and shrugs,
Her appeal falls flat as if they're wearing earplugs.
She has not come up with a plan B, she's enraged
Them, they're unimpressed by what she's staged.
The ERG thought 'no deal' would be her guide,
She's now said if her deal falls she'll let MPs decide.
      Since she's left the meeting four hours have passed in gloom.
280   She's sent a meal on a tray in her windowless room,
An office in the European Council's building.
She's declined the leaders' *langoustines* and duckling.
Just as a *koi* carp ignores feed floating

On its pond's surface, scarcely moves, hugging
The bottom, seeming to sulk, so May's ignored
The food sent out from the thoughtful leaders' board.
She's ordered pizza from a different menu.
To the leaders she's unreliable and through,
And has only a five-per-cent chance based on what she affirms
290   Of fulfilling Brexit on their agreed terms.
She has lost all her credibility,
The EU leaders debate, eventually
They give her not three months but just three weeks,
And set her Brexit timetable, which piques.
They grant an unconditional extension
To April the twelfth to get her deal won
Or for her, or Parliament, to say what will happen,
And if her deal's approved a further extension
To the twenty-second of May so legislation
300   Can be got through, and ratification.
     This is the last date she can have without fighting
The European elections, which would be sickening.
They've removed the 'no-deal' cliff edge from next week
And don't want to be blamed for a 'no deal' that's bleak.
The UK'll leave the EU on April
The twelfth if there's no deal unless it can still
Find another way out of the chaos next week,
Hold European elections and seek
A longer delay so all options – deal again,
310   'No deal', rethink, revoke – remain open
And the UK have three weeks to choose a new way
And Parliament could agree to revoke and stay.
     Their strategy's been to refuse to preview
A trade deal till the UK's left the EU
And offer a Withdrawal Agreement so
Pro-EU only a fool would swallow
It, and sit back and watch the infighting until
Brexit is stopped – you have to admire their skill.
May seems to grasp her deal has a doomed feel,

320   And seems reconciled to there being 'no deal'.
      May speaks at a press conference and makes it clear
    It's her deal or 'no deal', she won't hear
    Of a long extension and holding costly
    European elections and revoking Article 50.
    Juncker has said he has given three lots
    Of assurances, he can't undo any knots.
    The deal is closed, it's now up to the UK.
    A cross-party group will meet Barnier.
    Eighteen ministers plan to seize control

330   And vote on versions of Brexit, with one goal.
    There are multiple calls for May to resign,
    Her days look numbered, she is far from fine.
    She's failed to make the EU leaders bend.
    She goes to her Chequers bunker for the weekend.
    Captain and crew have wrecked the Ship of State
    And the engines judder – it's stuck on rocks – and grate.
    The Ship of State's survived peril, it's blessed.
    It's still intact, the mutiny suppressed.
    Now they've refloated the Ship, and it's on its way.

340   Lo! ahead's not paradise but its home bay.
    The Ship of State set out with hope to cross
    The dipping sea to a land of plenty and toss
    But found it was somehow back at the start,
    The harbour it sailed from with heavy heart.
    The Ship of Fools sails round and round to trail
    Back to where it started, where it set sail.
    The steerers had been steering how they thought,
    Ignoring stars and compasses, self-taught.

Canto XVI
Back towards Harbour

Sing, Muse, of fury as men came to see
Blocking May's deal lost their opportunity.
And sing of delays to Brexit, and of dismay.
Sing of extensions that came to feel like "Stay".
    Sunday at Chequers and all the headlines scream
That a right-wing *coup* against May has some steam.
May invites Brexiteers to a meeting
And pleads for support to get her deal moving.
They say the price is for her to step down.
Next day May says tells Parliament, with a frown,
There'll be no third Meaningful Vote as there's not support.
Letwin's amendment would control the agenda brought
On Wednesdays, the Government loses by twenty-seven
And three ministers resign. The MPs, then,
Have voted to take control of Brexit, the power
To decide Brexit's passed to the MPs, who glower.
It's said Letwin's plan amounts to a *coup*.
Who's behind it? Are Rothschilds turning the screw?
But the Withdrawal Agreement must be passed,
The only thing the EU wants to happen fast.
    And now May's meeting the 1922
Committee. Brady's told her she is through
And must go and in return her deal will be passed.
All are agog, how long will she now last?
Will she announce her departure's definite?
In Committee Room fourteen she says she'll quit
Earlier than she intended, before a second
Phase of Brexit negotiations is opened
So long as her deal is passed, she's trading the office
Of her premiership for votes, putting service
Before self. It's a *coup*. The ERG, it's said,
Are taking the party over and self-interested
Johnson will now vote for the deal he foul-mouthed and resigned

10

20

30

Over to get her out and himself in, blind,
By mid-July. To deliver Brexit she
Has fallen on her sword, another PM to be
Brought down by Europe, like Cameron. Some gloat
But now it's announced the DUP will vote
Against May's deal if it's brought back, it won't go through again,
40   And her conditional resignation's been in vain.
Will her resignation be revoked? Rivals
Are already stating policies like rebels.
She's resigned to get her deal through and it won't,
She can't even resign in a way fools don't.
      Sixteen indicative votes for Letwin's jiggery.
Eight are to be voted on simultaneously
When MPs control the agenda this way.
It's said Letwin's Prime Minister for the day.
Bercow reads out the numbers one by one.
50   There's no majority for any – none.
A second referendum has the most votes.
No one caucus will obtain what it promotes,
There has to be a compromise – don't mock.
The Commons has failed to break the deadlock,
It's now May's deal, which the EU'll accept,
Or no Brexit if her leadership's inept.
      Friday, the day of reckoning, the last day
To get a deal through, the day the UK
Was to leave the EU and there's no champagne,
60   Just a bitter taste of betrayal and great strain.
Friday, and the vote on the Withdrawal Agreement
Without the Political Declaration present
So it's not the same Agreement in the chamber
Voted on a third time and squeezed past the Speaker.
It cedes control and many MPs feel sore,
It's a deal that's signed after a defeat in war.
Labour and the DUP vote against and heave;
Rees-Mogg and Johnson vote for, just to leave.
Johnson said the deal creates "a vassal state",

70   But he's for it now it makes him a candidate.
Just as a fox that has entered a coop
And left hens' carcasses strewn around its snoop
Changes its ways and looks for friendliness,
So the ERG leadership found no caress.
    The votes are announced. May's deal's been defeated
Again by fifty-eight. Stricken, livid,
She says an alternative must now be found.
She's begged for her party's support and her deal's been drowned.
A long extension looms if there's a purpose:
80   To hold an election or people's vote caucus.
May's deal's not been passed despite her sacrifice
Of her premiership to reach her fools' paradise.
The Chequers plan has taken the Government
From leaving to a long extension and permanent
Remaining in the EU through a process
That's dumped May's premiership and brought distress.
Tusk tweets there'll be a European Council
Meeting in Brussels on the tenth of April,
Which will agree the way forward as the UK
90   Faces 'no deal' in just two weeks and may
Opt for a long extension as Robbins crowed
(After paying 5.3 billion that's owed
And implementing the backstop to make headway)
To April 2020's All Fools' Day.
But 'no deal' may be the outcome, and disdain,
And revoking Article 50 to remain.
Uncertainty is now a way of life
Along with anger at Parliamentary strife.
This Parliament can't get legislation through,
100   But it is there till 2022.
It's a Parliament of Fools that's a rabble,
And its paradise now looks delusional.
    All Fools' Day and none can tell the difference
Between Parliamentary farce and common sense.
Four more indicative votes that appeal

For a customs union, a Norway-style deal,
A people's vote and a revocation.
The Speaker reads the votes, it's a rejection.
All four have been defeated, sense 'no deal' loom
110   In eleven days' time. The fools are sunk in gloom.
They've not got beyond conflict to the unity
Behind all difference and diversity.
Where are the wise who can convey a harmonious view?
On the Ship of State there are few wise in the crew.
    The Ship of State is stuck upon the rocks.
A seven-hour Cabinet meeting and more shocks.
Fourteen Cabinet ministers back 'no deal',
And ten a customs union by feel
After the top civil servant Sedwill's lament
120   That 'no deal' will put food prices up ten per cent,
Depreciate sterling, make blocked credit rife,
Trigger company bail-outs and civil strife,
Disrupt defence and bring a hard border
That necessitates Direct Rule in Ulster
And so threatens the Union with doom.
    In a broadcast in an empty Downing-Street room
May surprisingly sides with the minority
And with Sedwill, and national unity,
To extend Article 50 till May
130   The twenty-second and, with Corbyn's say,
Will sail the Ship with a customs union's freight
So she can bring her Withdrawal Agreement straight
Back before the House – plus a customs union –
Without fighting the EU's election,
For "national unity" in the "national interest",
Squeezing a fourth vote past Bercow's strict test.
She's allied with a Marxist deemed till recently
A threat to national security,
And has declared war on her own party
140   And threatens to shift from her red lines, partly.

The mood in the ERG is truculent.
The Brexiteers have lost the argument.
It seems the end of Brexit, and Corbyn
Is being dragged in so he can be blamed by spin.
But he will win credit for trying to float
Brexit off the rocks and extend his popular vote.
The fools, wanting a perfect Brexit, voting
Against May's deal and greedily not thinking
Half a loaf is better than none, wanting the whole loaf

150   Or nothing, have missed the moment like any foolish oaf.
        A vote to have more indicative votes is afloat.
It's tied and lost on the Speaker's casting vote.
Now Cooper and Letwin's bill to force a long
Extension and head off 'no deal' as wrong
Wins by one vote and will now be debated.
It's rammed through Parliament in four hours, hurried
Into law in one night, a legally-
Binding vote on extending Article 50
If May's deal's not passed by the twelfth of April,

160   A blocking of 'no deal' that's pivotal.
There will now be a long extension for
Six months or even a year, or even more,
During which a future Government can revoke and undo
Article 50, and stay in the EU.
        And now Tusk proposes a flexible
Extension, "a flextension", for a year, durable
To the eve of 2020's All Fools' Day
With an early exit if the UK
Ratifies the Withdrawal Agreement before,

170   As the EU don't want to keep agreeing more.
May wants a short extension to the end of June,
And will prepare for the European elections soon.
At Wednesday's Council all will become clear.
For the UK may not leave for another year
And Robbins' words in the Brussels bar were sane.
It's a never-ending leaving that will remain.

May's opting for cross-party talks (after
The seven-hour Cabinet meeting) has stunned. Labour
Say May's not compromised on her red lines.
180   They're waiting for a customs union's signs
(Not called that) with a legally-binding
Lock requested by Labour preventing
A future PM from unpicking it,
So there may be a fourth Meaningful Vote to commit
To the Withdrawal Agreement and Political
Declaration plus a customs union's bundle,
Ratification subject to a confirmatory
Referendum with an option to stay in immediately,
And an extension to the end of June –
190   To leave on the twenty-second of May, soon,
To shun the European elections that she has despised.
She's asked for Labour's help as Tusk advised
And is taking revenge on the blocking ERG
Who fear she'll give Corbyn credibility
So he ends up in Downing Street, inheriting.
She may be running down the clock and threatening
Her MPs with voting for her deal or
Facing a long extension, at Labour's door.
    Her party and donors are incandescent,
200   Activists are on strike and are truculent.
May says it's her deal or never leaving.
Jenkin says staying-in's better than accepting
The vassalage of May's deal, and its cost.
If the Government falls Brexit will be lost.
The EU – France, Belgium, Austria and Spain –
Don't want any extension, it's now plain,
As the UK may, in Rees-Mogg's words, veto
The EU's budget, obstruct its army – oh, no –
And block Macron's integrationist schemes.
210   The UK's future will be determined, it seems,
By the twenty-seven EU member states
Regardless of what May and Labour propose (and the Fates).

But now there's a prospect the UK will change its mind
And choose to stay in the EU and be kind.
    The European Council summit looms sullen,
Will it grant the UK a short or long extension?
Macron wants short, Tusk long, both fail to cheer.
There's an idea it would be to the end of the year
With reviews every three months, and the UK
220   Would be in an airlock, unable to waylay
Budget talks and trade deals as it waits to be free.
It would be like the UK "being in Purgatory".
May meets Merkel in Berlin and then Macron
In Paris. She presses her case, and then is gone.
To avoid 'no deal' in two days May can go for broke.
It's like the nuclear button, only she can revoke.
    The day of the Brussels Council meeting
Of the twenty-seven, it's sunny, the sea's sparkling.
May gives a presentation for an hour
230   For an extension to the end of June, all glower.
(A hundred and seventy-seven of her MPs – wow –
Voted against any extension now.)
The twenty-seven are irritated and under strain,
Summoned to an emergency meeting for Brexit again.
She's left and they're discussing what to say.
The EU's in control, not the UK.
A leak, seventeen support a long extension,
Four including France a shorter one – stubborn
Macron's said "We have a European Renaissance
240   To run and don't want the UK's blocking presence" –
And the EU'll demand that the UK will not mess
With the bloc's decision-making process.
    Now the result: a delay until Hallowe'en,
October the thirty-first, the 'trick or treat' scene,
With a review at the end of June to reckon
And assess the UK's co-operation.
It's a "flextension" for six months, and so
Can be terminated earlier if the UK can go.

Tusk says to the British, "Please don't waste this time."
250 May's furious party thinks she's committed a crime.
The talks with Labour show no compromise,
The Withdrawal Agreement won't pass, even in disguise.
Planning for 'no deal' has already, by Sedwill, been stopped:
1.5 billion spent, till October no plan to adopt.
She can't leave before the European elections, anyhow.
Parliament's deadlocked, it's an election now.
Her party's seething, it's time for her to go.
But that'd waste time, it's a people's vote that'll show
The way forward from all this disarray
260 And solve all the current problems with a loud "Stay".
    Now a poll says the Tories will lose fifty-nine seats.
They've no message and their Brexit's been full of defeats.
They want to change the rules to get May out quickly.
They think a new leader'll rig a majority
And go for 'no deal', but there'd be a hung Parliament
And 'no deal' is not going to happen, that's self-evident.
A general election could let Corbyn in
To unleash Marxism on all, and ruin.
Labour's hugely ahead in the polls and could hold
270 A second referendum. Brexit could fold.

May's pact with Labour is not doable,
And her fourth attempt to get the Withdrawal
Agreement passed has been blocked by the Cabinet,
Who won't sanction a new referendum yet.
She's barricaded herself inside Downing Street
For two days, and has now agreed to meet
The 1922 Committee's clout
(Whose private exit poll's warned of a near wipe-out
In the European elections). She's just made
280 A speech outside number ten's door, her stockade.
She's agreed to resign on the seventh of June
And stay until her successor can commune.
She's tearful, and her voice cracks as she ends.

She's failed to win support, she's without friends.
She's left no legacy, she's been the worst PM:
A Remainer who changed to Leave as a stratagem
To advance her career, to subordinate
Her beliefs to delivering Brexit, after a wait.
She's been opportunistic and has clung to power.
290   It's all ended in tears in just an hour.
     She leaves behind a polarised country,
More support 'Stay in' than 'Leave', it's binary.
The middle way is now unpopular,
'Compromise' is now a reviled word, a slur.
In the European elections the Tories
Have won just four seats and come fifth. It is
The Tories' worst election result to-do
Since the Reform Act of 1832.
The party system's now broken, May's deal,
300   The Chequers plan, has killed Tories' appeal.
The one-issue Brexit party will push
For a 'no deal' in a disastrous ambush.
Johnson circles with a rapacious shark's eyes.
O Hermes, please can we vote to ostracise
A public menace to remotest Syria?
May's finished, her deal's dead, what a failure.
The EU won't change the Withdrawal Agreement,
Which has the force of a treaty, of bound intent.
It's 'no deal' – banned by Parliament and cursed –
310   Or 'Revoke and stay in', on October the thirty-first.
     Now May is a sad and tragic figure, that's plain.
She's grovelled to the EU again and again.
A Remainer who led hard men and had to be nice,
She survived by supporting their delusional paradise.
If she had thought at the start 52:48
Meant a soft Brexit, not a hard 'no deal' with hate,
Then the country would not be as divided
As it is now, it would be united.
She's gone along with the Chequers plan that's lost

320   Her premiership, a pyrrhic victory, and cost.
The plan has dumped out all the Brexiteers –
Davis, Johnson, Raab, now May – and's ended in tears.
She believed she had a democratic duty
To deliver an epoch-defining policy
That she believed was not in the national interest,
Because referendum voters thought it best;
And she'll be remembered for her catastrophic
Mishandling of the negotiations, for her quick
Triggering of Article 50 without a plan,

330   For boxing herself within red lines that ban,
For accepting the EU's sequencing,
For her secretive Chequers compromising,
For an election which lost her majority,
For pledging thirty-nine billion pounds too promptly
Without any trade agreement, for ignoring
The forty-eight per cent who were worrying,
For obstinately pushing the Withdrawal
Agreement with a backstop that's been trouble,
Then trashing it and seeking to reopen

340   It, leaving the EU bemused again;
And for taking the UK to the brink of 'no deal'
To scare her MPs into voting 'real'.
She and her circle have not understood
How the EU works, she has thought she could
Deal directly with the EU leaders
And go behind the backs of the Sherpas –
Institutional heads and bureaucrats who engage –
And divide and rule as in the imperial age,
Prioritise goods over services

350   Which bring in eighty per cent of the UK's riches
In a fantasy of release and liberation
When the UK'll live in endless negotiation.
     Yet to some her waiting game has been sly
And outfoxed her ultras who've sought 'no deal' by
Voting against her deal and more moderate way

And have inflicted on their Brexit a long delay.
She's faced them with backing her deal or opposing
It and risking Brexit not happening.
There's been a long extension as Robbins said
360   In the Brussels bar, and she has won, though 'dead',
A strategic victory by feline statecraft
And outmanoeuvred her ultras without being daft
And splitting the Conservative party,
Focusing on her party, not her country.
But Remainers barely featured in her soft deal
And have otherwise been ignored amid the zeal.
Her deal, a second-best, limited damage
And the next-best was a long extension package
That could turn into staying-in along the way
370   And participating in a new heyday,
A United States of Europe with the reach
Churchill foresaw in his post-war Zurich speech,
In the European civilisation's union stage.
And your poet, who lived at a young age
In Churchill's constituency during the war,
Perpetuates Churchill's vision and saw,
And now confirms, the UK's civilisation's the European,
And no nation's ever left its own civilisation.
    It's the end of an era in the UK,
380   An era of looking outwards without dismay,
Intervening in Europe's crises, standing firm on the law
Against Soviet occupation in the Cold War
When Europe was divided, bringing harmony
To a warring continent for seventy
Years. Now how wretched the UK seems, a flop
On promises, unable to solve the backstop,
Diminished and in decline, parading weakness.
O Palmerston, what would you make of this mess?
Your poet sadly reflects, nearly in tears,
390   That he's charted the decline in verse for sixty years
And, "the poet of decline", flag at half-mast,

He now laments a greatness that has passed.
O Churchill, how rueful you'd be at your world role's decrease
And the lack of vision to implement world peace.
Johnson and Hunt have both received *World State*
But their world-view is limited to the fate
Of the nation-state, not humanity. They've not shone.
O Blake and Shelley, where has the vision gone?
Only your poet shines on a world state now,
400   Only your poet keeps the vision going somehow.

Cut off from the rest of the world, fractious,
All went along with the circuitous
Voyage, all on the Ship of State had no clue,
Are collectively culpable – both crew
And passengers, all who nominate
The tribunes they voted for to create
This mess. The majority are revealed
As a muddling lot of mainly well-heeled
Stultified fools. *Stultifera navis*,
410   The simpletons acted from a premiss
And failed to see their actions would consign
Their country into a massive decline,
Not one of the more glorious episodes
In their country's grand history, demanding odes
Of celebration for a great triumph.
Somewhere on the Ship of State wise men harrumph
And, though there will be twists and turns and a rout
As mutineers seize power and are then forced out,
They chart a new course that leads to a land
420   Where true Paradise can be glimpsed and planned.
Meanwhile new mutineers have seized the wheel
And steer for a paradise that to them is real
But fills dismayed wise men with deep unease:
A fools' paradise where money grows on trees.

Epilogue
True Paradise

Sing, Muse, of the gods, and of how Zeus foresaw
The way forward for divided nations' law,
Sing of Zeus's thinking and his sedate,
Far-sighted vision of a new World State.
Sing his concern for humankind's prospects,
And his yearning for a World State's projects.
And sing of how Zeus struggled to understand
Humankind's way forward now, that can't be planned
Because of the free will all humans live by,
Sing of the lack of progress that made him sigh.
    In exasperation with the UK's leader,
On Olympus Zeus frowned amid thunder.
He had lost patience with the UK's dithering,
And then the Meaningful Vote's delaying.
"British politicians are all useless," he complained.
He fulminated, "They've been stuck and chained
In a static situation of backstop.
I'm fed up with the lot of them." Quite a strop.
"They're just a Ship of Fools who don't know where
They're going." He sought out Hermes in despair.
And grumbled: "The British are so slow, they're paralysed.
It's painful to wait while their free will's exercised.
You know I'm trying to bring peace and a goal
To the divided world the UN can't control.
The EU's done a good job pacifying
Europe, which was devastated and expiring
In chaos seventy-five years ago,
All war-damaged, today you'd never know.
And just when we thought we were winning, mess again:
Putin invaded Crimea and stirred up Ukraine
And pestered the EU's eastern borders, and, split,
The UK turned nationalistic and voted to exit
The EU and trumpet independence,

10

20

30

And as if that wasn't enough – it's got no sense –
The US chose an isolationist President
Who pulled out of the Paris Agreement,
The UN Framework Convention on Climate Change,
Started trade wars and now wants to arrange
For a wall to be built to shut out Mexico
40   When we want walls pulled down, not erected. You know
I'm dragging the UN's nation-states, too late,
Kicking and screaming into a peaceful World State
But the dragon of nationalism's everywhere:
Armed men rise from sown teeth bent on warfare
In seventy-two wars. As I often say,
Where there are nation-states war is not far away.
Limited supranationalism will bind
In their best interests stupid humankind
Who can't seem to organise living in peace
50   Without intervention by us gods above Greece.
Macron's spoken against nationalism's traits.
He's set to work to bring in a United States
Of Europe that's fully integrated
With fifty states, the stepping-stone we tread
To a World State. But what's the immediate
Way forward? Is it for the British to submit,
And become a vassal state with a humble view,
A colony of the expanding EU?
Is it for the EU to teach the UK a lesson?
60   You've been doing things on earth, where have they gone?"
Just as a grandfather who has lived long
Sees an alien world that looks all wrong
Compared with what he knew back in his youth,
So Zeus looked on a world now short of truth
And looked down on recalcitrant humankind
In uncomprehending sorrow that it is so blind.

    Hermes replied: "O Lord of all, I can confide,
I've been working on our plan. I have got inside
The minds of Juncker and Barnier and have fed

70   The idea Robbins should be their spearhead
And they have produced the Withdrawal Agreement,
Which, as we planned, has been bungled and's compliant
As it's a compromise, half in, half out,
And is loathed by everyone, without a doubt.
I have fed Grieve's and Bercow's discontent
And the stage is set for the UK Parliament
To request a second referendum, hooray.
I've tried to feed ideas to the mind of May
To revoke Article 50, but her mind

80   Was not receptive, her imagination's blind.
I wasn't getting very far. But anyway,
There is a good chance the UK will stay
In the EU. As for the US's reach,
I am urging the Democrats to impeach
Their President and drum him from office.
There's been a Government shutdown and I promise
There'll soon be a move to retrieve America.
A World State's a long way off in the future.
We can only proceed one step at a time."

90   Zeus groaned and said impatiently: "But I'm
In favour of a World State now. It's too slow.
You said the man who wrote *World State* would know
The way forward to a World State. He's wise,
I managed to meet him when in disguise
I entered a garden statue of me.
He said he's grasped the Law of History,
The stages of each civilisation,
That Europe's current stage is its Union.
Find him and ask him what needs to happen now,

100   How we get to a World State from here. How?"
      Alas, the gods are as devoid of vision
As all the politicians, whose passion
They reflect. Zeus may be omnipotent,
But he's grown old and can't see how to implement,
Let alone guide, humankind's step-by-step fate,

Its progress to a universal World State.
As an old, doddery elder statesman fades,
He's lost his insight into coming decades;
And the gods beneath him are as full of dissent
110   As the UK's Cabinet, they all have different
Emphases and squabble, but like a nurse
Apollo's Light nurtures the universe
And Zeus's goddess of wisdom, Minerva,
Is loyal as is Hermes, his messenger.
Zeus, like May, finds it hard to keep control.

And so Hermes appeared as if out for a stroll
(Curly-haired and bearded, like a traveller,
No wings on his feet or staff, just a saunterer)
Near your poet's white bust of Apollo,
120   Climbed his spiral stair, tapped on his window –
As does a parakeet in cold weather
To request more nuts in the bird feeder –
And beckoned him out on the balcony.
    Your poet was communing contemplatively
With the Light that keeps the universe fertile
And joined him in mild air with a warm smile
And stood like a stag with seven-branched antlers
Quite still between two worlds above his pastures
And said: "Hello again, how have things been going?"
130   Hermes said, "I know what you've been writing,
I've looked over your shoulder when you've bent in gloom,
And I've leafed through your work when you've left your room.
Your poem is like a many-pieced jigsaw
That sees all sides of a complex civil war.
You've held your mirror up to society
And have reflected chaos tellingly.
Truth can be found in your sixteen cantos, yes –
Your dissection of the UK's current mess –
And in your twenty-five civilisations' pattern
140   And in what your *Rise and Fall* tables discern,

Which our gods have all read. It helps us understand
The dreadful things that are happening in each land.
We know you're going to Russia to explain
How a World State can disarm so peace can reign,
And how a universal peace can bring
A prosperous world and end all suffering.
Your speech will found a new era of peace
On the first day of the year of the phoenix, when wars cease,
Which in the Mayan calendar comes round
150   Every two thousand years, and was last renowned
Just after the rise of Augustus's Roman Empire,
And will now, on April the twenty-second, inspire
The rise of your Universalist World State.
Zeus has arranged for you to receive an ornate
Golden phoenix rising from the embers
Of nation-states as a World State recurs.
Zeus wants to know how we get to a World State now.
He wants the UK to stay in the EU somehow
And use its vision to shape a new world.
160   You have a role in revealing what's to be unfurled.
But we're especially interested in Europe
And how its civilisation will develop.
Zeus wants to know what will happen now, you feel,
To the UK? Will it crash out to 'no deal'?
Or remain in the EU and work for peace
After a second referendum's release?"
    Your poet had several times been transported
To the gods while channelling cantos the Muses fed,
And knew loyal Tennyson, who he first met at night
170   In Farringford House on the Isle of Wight
And who now frequents his study, feeds words from his chair
And when your poet wakes floats through the air
Amendments to yesterday's lines, to be reset,
Acting as editor. And so your poet
Was used to gods and Muses communing,
A gift that comes with metaphysical living

When the soul is as still as a puddle, or a pond,
And reflects the Light that shines like the sun from beyond,
So it was normal that Hermes should drop by
180   Like an old friend passing from the Olympian sky.

They descended the stair to the terrace below
And your poet said, standing by Apollo
(Speaking in trance like the Delphic Oracle,
The Pythia, the High Priestess in the Temple
Of Apollo, through whom Apollo spoke):
"The chaotic UK's become a joke.
The Law of History is clear, no nation
Can 'walk out' of its own civilisation.
The UK will remain in the EU
190   Although I have to say that point of view
Has looked unlikely till now. I see beyond this mess,
And beyond this Government's recklessness
That's put democracy and sovereignty
Above the economy and unity.
An example will be made of its flawed view.
    "Europe will not concede much, the EU
Does not want the UK to do better than
Its twenty-seven other members, its plan
Is to send a message to all that secession's not grand,
200   But disastrous. The EU needs to expand
Into a United States of Europe, so
With the United States of America it can show
A United States of the Pacific the date
They can all draw together into one World State.
Throughout Europe, the US and the world
Supranationalism has been challenged and churled
By nationalism. Defeating Brexit and Trump
Will set back nationalism with a hefty thump.
And accelerate progress to a World State
210   That will unify humankind and end hate.
    "How to get there? You'll have to read what *World State*'s faced.

It's all in there, a World State at first based
In the UN General Assembly, all
The constituencies a World State needs, the call.
Macron is right, the EU needs its own defence,
The UK has to accept that this makes sense,
That the way forward is to stay in the EU,
Which it has not yet left. Brexiteers, it's true,
Have been exposed as breaking their promises.

220   They lured the electorate with fantasies
And undeliverable hopes that were steals:
More cash for the NHS, instant trade deals.
None of these can happen except by borrowing.
There'll be no dividend from exiting.
The Brexiteers have continually, like fools,
Underestimated the EU's rules.
We have seen this fantasy Brexit unravel:
The UK alone, trading with the world of travel
As in the days when the British Empire

230   Ruled a quarter of the world and taught it to aspire.
That's a dream, the UK's means are now limited;
A fools' paradise, where happiness is founded
On an illusion and's not unlike fool's gold
Which proved to be iron pyrites and unsold.
We have seen the wreck of that global counterfeit
Britannia, the wreck of Brexit: Wrexit.
      "The EU'll stand firm. 'No deal'? All shudder and frown.
Parliament's voted the Chequers plan down,
The Withdrawal Agreement's not been ratified,

240   Parliament's paralysed, and MPs' hands are tied,
And with a no-confidence vote defeated
And a general election avoided,
There'll somehow be a second referendum
With a choice between a long Brexit or the plum,
'No Brexit', staying in the EU: a backtrack.
The vote'll one day be to remain, the UK'll be back
Where it started but may lose the Major opt-out

From the social chapter and the Thatcher rebate and clout.
It'll be worse off financially, need a loan,
250   And it may be asked to join the eurozone.
It's all been a lot of huffing and puffing
To be back where we started with less good terms, struggling,
Four billion pounds wasted on preparing to leave,
Weaving a pattern we now have to unweave.
And the Brexiteers will be vilified and will reel.
They'll be seen as having grabbed the steering-wheel
Of the Ship of State and steered the people on
To the rocks, talking of land on the horizon
Excitedly but unable to say
260   What's there. They will be regarded with dismay,
As raising deception to a higher level
In politics than there's ever been: that of 'scoundrel'.
They've been living in a fools' paradise,
Where they've been heading's as wonderful as ice,
But they don't know in what way, or how to get there.
They've persuaded a people to sail into a nightmare,
And delivery will be when the Ship of Fools returns
To where it started, the safe harbour for which it yearns.
    "International politics has been riven by
270   A dialectic between connectivity
And isolation; supranationalism,
And nationalism which has not been welcome,
And the managing of Brexit's tipped the balance
In favour of supranationalism's presence
Throughout the rest of the world. The containment
Of Brexit's crucial to progress and assent
To a coming World State as the attack
Of nationalism will have received a set-back.
    "Out of this mess will come good. And I can see
280   A World State in which the UK and the EU will be
Integrated as integral partners, joyous,
United in a peaceful and prosperous
Paradise that makes our present world seem

Like a Hell of humans torturing every dream,
Starving bellies and breaking limbs everywhere
With explosions on the ground and from the air.
The universe is full of different things
That compete and clash, that crawl and flutter wings.
All opposites are held within the One
290   As our solar system is held within the sun.
Rest assured, all Brexit questions angrily hurled
Will be resolved in a united world
    "'No deal' has been ruled out, the UK won't be leaving.
But uncertainty will last years, and questioning.
May and her deal have been thrown overboard,
There can be long extensions and more discord.
A vote of no confidence in the Government
Can sink the lot of them, if it's provident.
But Article 50's run its course, the hour chimes.
300   Your poet's run out of perspectives, and rhymes.
The Ship of State's safe, and on its homeward run.
It's time for me to leave the stage. I'm done."
    Hermes nodded and said, "Thanks. Avoiding the brink's....
I'll pass it on to Zeus. It's what he thinks."
(Leaders steal ideas and claim they're their own.)
"We're grateful you've set down all you have known
About the progress of the Chequers plan.
You have higher consciousness, and you can
See the past flows into future as the estuary
310   Of a river widens as it approaches the sea.
You can see the future will flow from where it's reached now."
    Your poet nodded, peering with a furrowed brow.
"All history and contemporary affairs
Is one process, and where you stand ensnares
And cuts the flow to you into past, present
And future. And you know that each event
To come flows from what has been already.
We gods have just one goal, the unity
Of all humankind, which can only flow

320 From the process that passes us now as we who know
Look ahead. But like the Delphic Oracle
You speak enigmatically within a riddle.
True Paradise is ahead, if we can bring
It to birth. We gods are always interpreting
Coded riddles that convey Reality,
Gleams from the Light, the One behind each galaxy,
What Apollo's seen and sent from Zeus's mind:
A World State uniting all humankind."
  And, standing next to Apollo, your poet sensed
330 A shadow pass between him and the sun, and tensed,
And he was alone by the winding spiral stair.
The gods know their limitations and work in air
To fulfil their noble ambitions and concern
For undeserving humankind that must learn
To subordinate selfish and nationalistic instincts
To the greater good of a united humanity's precincts.

In your poet's Cornish harbour, the sparkling sea
Washes to shore, laps nuzzling boats fondly.
Your poet rests in tranquillity between
340 Headlands, and from his window surveys the scene,
A peaceful nook where a soul can bud to a bard
And bloom and fade, then lie in the churchyard.
Your poet is at peace, his work's finished.
He lets his mind wander the sea as it's wished
And now it's free to roam, the discipline
Of rhyming couplets ended, and can imagine.
Reality can be known by a receptive mind
Like a vast ocean where a gull soars looking to find.
The Ship of Fools ploughs back, a group of seers
350 Have mutinied against the mutineers.
The captain and some crew now know where they
Are going, but paradise seems far away.
  There is a true Paradise that's too far
In the future, like a horizon's star,

For the ship to sail into its calm harbour
And berth with its perfect new world order.
Please note, there's a good New World Order that would rule
Through a democratic World State and school,
And there's a bad New World Order that loots
360   All oil and gas in air wars and transmutes
And criss-crosses the earth with pipelines strewn
Through conquered states for their personal fortune:
The syndicate of *élite* families
That steal the earth's resources for their ease.
But it is a law that cannot be broken
That a nation can't leave its own civilisation.
Over the waves true Paradise shimmers
With tremulous light, distant haze that stirs.
Sail closer, true Paradise shimmers in sun,
370   One World State, democratically run
With all humankind represented in law
And no more nuclear weapons or war,
No famine, disease or poverty there,
Both finance and the environment now fair,
All Leavers and Remainers now at one,
All conflicts reconciled under the sun,
All civilisations internally
Themselves but externally in harmony,
A Paradise where all humankind can
380   Live at peace at one as in Zeus's plan
That was undermined by the self-interest
Of some leaders so humankind regressed,
But such fallen let-downs can be reversed
As the good triumph over the selfish worst
As a mutinous ship returns to its wharf's berth,
And Paradise can return to the earth.

7 August 2018 – 29 May 2019

Timeline
Main events of the UK's attempt to leave the EU, in relation to the 16 cantos of *Fools' Paradise*

Date	Event	Canto
23 June 2016	UK Referendum, UK votes to leave the European Union	
29 March 2017	Theresa May triggers Article 50 via a hand-delivered letter	
8 June 2017	The UK Government loses its majority following a General Election	
7 July 2018	Chequers proposal is laid before Cabinet at Chequers	Canto I
8 July 2018	Resignation of David Davis as Brexit Secretary	Canto II
9 July 2018	Resignation of Boris Johnson as Foreign Secretary; appointment of Dominic Raab as Secretary for Exiting the EU	Canto II
12–15 July 2018	Donald Trump's visit to the UK	Canto III
16 July 2018	May concedes on four ERG amendments, killing Chequers plan	Canto IV
3 August 2018	May meets Emmanuel Macron at Fort de Brégançon	Canto V

23 August, 13 September 2018	UK Government publishes technical notices on how to prepare for a 'no-deal' Brexit	Canto VI
18–19 September 2018	Leaked Tory dossier reveals secret plan to replace May	Canto VII
19–20 September 2018	Salzburg informal summit for EU leaders	Canto VIII
3 October 2018	Conservative Party Conference	Canto IX
17 October 2018	Brussels summit, EU Council meeting	Canto X
25 November 2018	Brussels summit, EU Council meeting	Canto XI
13–14 December 2018	Brussels summit, EU Council meeting	Canto XII
19 January 2019	May loses first Meaningful Vote by 230 votes	Canto XIII
20 February 2019	May meets Jean-Claude Juncker in Brussels to try to change Withdrawal Agreement	Canto XIV
12 March 2019	May loses second Meaningful Vote by 149 votes	Canto XV
21 March 2019	Brussels summit, EU Council meeting: May is given an extension of Article 50 to 12 April and if her deal is approved a further extension to 22 May for ratification	Canto XV

29 March 2019	May loses third Meaningful Vote by 58 votes	Canto XVI
29 March 2019	UK due to leave the EU, extension granted	
10 April 2019	Brussels summit, EU Council meeting: May asks for extension to Article 50 until 30 June and is given extension until 31 October	Canto XVI
26 May 2019	Conservatives win only 4 out of 70 seats in the European elections	Canto XVI
7 June 2019	Official end of May's premiership following her resignation	Canto XVI
31 October 2019	UK scheduled to leave the EU	
31 January 2020	UK rescheduled to leave the EU	

BOOKS

O-BOOKS

O is a symbol of the world, of oneness and unity; this eye represents knowledge and insight.